Paris

Travel Guide

Etienne Carter

Table of Contents

INTRODUCTION

For centuries, Paris, the City of Light, has been a significant cultural center. This is where civilization peaked in art, fashion, gastronomy, literature, and intellectual pursuits. Embrace this city with a passion for its own culture, which is different from any other on earth, and you cannot help but capture the essence of romance and joie de vivre that makeup Paris.

Walk along the expansive boulevards of Paris; visit vibrant farmers' markets; or get lost in their world-renowned art galleries. You may have thinkers' café crème at a sidewalk café followed by an immersion into the beauty of a tree-lined park looking like an Impressionist painting. At the Louvre, you will encounter the Mona Lisa's enigmatic smile and the timeless beauty of Venus de Milo. Also, at the Orsay Museum, admire Monet and Renoir's works. Take a scenic cruise down the Seine, climb to the top of the Eiffel Tower, or just walk down Champs-Elysées Avenue. Keep your energies for the evening to fully experience one of the most romantic cities in the world.

Paris By Neighborhood

Central Paris (population 2.3 million) is demarcated by a ring road and bisected by the Seine River, which flows from east to west. The right bank of the Seine, called Rive Droite, lies in its northern part, whereas Rive Gauche, or Left Bank, is on its south side. Notre Dame, the bull's eye of Paris, stands on an island located right at the heart of the city.

The city is divided into twenty arrondissements (administrative districts) that are like a spiral of a snail shell leading out from the center. When you see a hotel with a zip code having 75007 as its last two digits, it falls under this district. A good number of Metros are within Paris, and many locals use them for travel purposes. For instance, according to Parisian references, the Eiffel Tower is situated on la Rive Gauche (the Left Bank) in the 7ème arrondissement, with the zip code being 75007 and le Métro Trocadéro as le plus proche.

Think about major landmarks in each neighborhood that comprises Paris.

Historic Core

This area focuses on the Ile de la Cité ("Island of the City"), situated in the middle of the Seine. Here, you will find some of Paris' most ancient sites, such as Roman ruins along with medieval Notre-Dame and Sainte-Chapelle churches. Other attractions include the Conciergerie, Archaeological Crypt, Deportation Memorial, riverside promenade, Les Plages de Paris Beaches, and the little Isle-St-Louis. Paris' historic riverside booksellers, known as les bouquinistes, line both sides of the Ile de la Cité as it flows through the city center.

Major Museums Neighborhood

This area is located just towards the west of the ancient city, and it is occupied by the Louvre, Orsay, and Orangerie museums. Other places to see include the Tuileries Garden and the Palais Royal Courtyards.

Champs-Elysées

A most famous avenue of 19th-century Right Bank Paris, extending north-west from Place de la Concorde to Arc de Triomphe, this is a place to visit. Below the area are Petit and Grand Palais, Hyatt Regency Paris Etoile (for a stunning view of the city), and La Défense with La Grande Arche.

Eiffel Tower Neighborhood

Eiffel Tower dominates, but it also includes lively Rue Cler with its hotels and restaurants, as well as the Army Museum & Napoleon's Tomb, Rodin Museum, etc. Besides that, one would find the Paris Sewer Museum or Marmottan Museum.

Opéra Neighborhood

The right bank upmarket district focuses on Opéra Garnier, featuring large boulevards while boasting distinctive sites too. Exclusive shopping can be done at the Galeries Lafayette department store; the Fragonard Perfume Museum has also been added there, as has the Jacquemart-André Museum, an elegant Opéra Garnier, in addition to other stalls around the Place Vendôme/Place de la Madeleine rubric.

Highlights of the City of Light

✦ ✦ ✦ **The Louvre**: The Mona Lisa's and Venus de Milo's abodes Hours: Wednesday to Monday, 9:00 to 18:00, closed Tuesdays.

✦ ✦ ✦ **Sainte-Chapelle**: This is a Gothic jewel that is famous for its stunning stained glass. Operating hours: Every day 09:00–19:00, October until March closes at 17:00.

✦ ✦ ✦ **Notre-Dame Cathedral**: Paris' most beloved cathedral, is no longer open indefinitely.

✦ ✦ ✦ **Eiffel Tower**: Daily in mid-June-August from 9 a.m.–24 p.m., September–mid-June from 9.30 a.m.–11.45 p.m.

✦ ✦ ✦ **Versailles**: The ultimate palace of kings with Mirrors Hall, extensive gardens, and a hamlet of the queen. Timetable: Château Tuesday-Sunday 9 a.m.–6 p.m.; Domaine du Trianon/Domaine Tuesday–Sunday 12 p.m.–6.30 p.m.; Gardens generally every day from 8 a.m. until half-past eight; November–March until six o'clock; Monday closed throughout the year.

✦ ✦ **Orsay Museum**: Illuminating art of the nineteenth century, featuring Europe's best Impressionist collection. Opening time: From Tuesday to Sunday inclusive (Wednesdays till nine forty-five pm), Monday off.

✦ ✦ ✦ **Champs-Elysées**: Paris's most renowned street extending from Place de la Concorde to Arc de Triomphe.

Orangerie Museum: This is where you'll find Monet's water lilies, among other masterpieces of modernism. Opening times: Wednesday to Monday (Tuesday closed) from nine o'clock in the morning to six o'clock in the evening.

Pompidou Centre: Modern art in a vibrant, colorful building with city views. Opening hours: Wed-Mon 11 am-9 pm, closed on Tues.

Riverside Promenades and Paris Plages: No cars allowed zones along the river for strolling and summer "beaches." Operating hours: Promenades: always open; Plages: from the middle of July to the middle of August, from 8:00 a.m. until midnight

Opéra Garnier: A dazzling Belle Époque theater with Chagall's ceiling. Hours: Mostly every day from 10 a.m. until 4 p.m. From mid-July to August, it is open until five p.m.

Rue Cler: The classic Parisian market street. Timetable: Shops are open from Tuesday to Saturday (8:30 am to 1 pm; 3 pm to 7.30 pm), Sunday (8:30 am to noon), with the later part of Sunday being quiet, and all day Monday when shops are closed.

Jacquemart-André Museum: An art-filled mansion from nineteenth-century France. Hours: Open every day from ten in the morning to six o'clock at night, while during special exhibits it closes at eight-thirty on Mondays.

Army Museum and Napoleon's Tomb: housing the grand tomb of Emperor Napoleon and extensive war exhibits. Timing: Open daily from ten in the morning to six in the evening; Napoleon's tomb opens until nine at night on Tuesdays.

Rodin Museum: Celebrating great sculptor's works within a peaceful garden setting. Operating hours: Every day except Monday, between ten o'clock in the morning and half past six p.m.

Père Lachaise Cemetery: Last resting place of many famous residents of Paris Hours: Monday-Friday, 8 a.m.–6 p.m.; Saturday, starting at half past eight; Sunday, beginning at nine a.m. but closing at half past five in winter.

Cluny Museum: Medieval art is showcased here, and it has the world-famous unicorn tapestries. Hours: Tuesday to Sunday (first and third Thursdays until 9 p.m.), closed on Mondays.

Arc de Triomphe: This is the first structure that one encounters while going through the Champs-Elysées. Working hours: Inside every day from ten o'clock till eleven p.m., October-March till then thirty p.m.

Marmattan Museum: Concentration on Monet Art. Hours: Tuesday to Sunday 10:00–6:00 pm, Thursday until 9:00 pm, closed on Monday.

Carnavalet Museum: 16th-century mansion housing Paris' past. Hours: Tuesday-Sunday 10:00-6:00 pm, closed Mondays.

Montmartre and Sacré-Cœur: This is a bohemian hilltop district with the most beautiful white basilica and great views. Hours:

Every day from 6.30 a.m. until 10.30 p.m.; Dome climb daily from 10 a.m. until 8 p.m.; Oct.-May until 6 p.m.; Jan.-Feb.-till five o'clock in the evening.

Panthéon: A classical monument where some important people are buried. The hours are daily from 10:00 a.m. to 6:30 p.m.; from October to March, at six o'clock in the evening.

Picasso Museum: Roaming exhibits of Picasso's art in a three-floor building. Hours: Tue-Fri at.30 am–6 pm, Sat-Sun from 9 am closed on Monday.

Planning your Trip

These proposed day plans show how much one well-organized, motivated, and coffee-high visitor can see. Don't overschedule—save some surprises for another trip. A week is great for a Paris getaway. If you have less than a week, select from the suggested itineraries below.

Day 1: Start with the Historical Walk of Paris, featuring Notre Dame, the Latin Quarter, and Sainte-Chapelle. Then take a rest in Luxembourg Garden before visiting Cluny Museum and exploring Opéra Garnier. Finish your day with a river Seine boat cruise at night.

Day 2: Tour the Louvre in the morning. Walk along Champs-Elysées from Arc de Triomphe to Tuileries Garden and consider visiting the Orangerie Museum. Dinner on Ile St. Louis was followed by a floodlit walk near Notre Dame.

Day 3: Begin with trips to Orsay and Rodin Museums. After lunch, visit the Army Museum as well as Napoleon's Tomb nearby. Take a stroll around the Rue Cler area, sit down in a café or two, and relax at this point of your trip in Paris before moving on to finish with the Left Bank riverside promenade walk and evening bus/taxi/retro car tour.

Day 4: Take RER/Train-C to Versailles; go through palace interiors, etc. Have lunch there, then check out other sights in the palace before coming back to Paris for dinner.

Day 5: Concentrate on the Marais district and visit C!|arnavalet. Have lunch at Place des Vosges or Rue des Rosiers. Choose any place from Marais sights: Pompidou Centre, Jewish Art & History Museum, Picasso Museum, or Père Lachaise Cemetery—not all of them though! Ride the Eiffel Tower at sunset and go up Trocadéro afterward.

Day 6: Either make a day trip outside, such as to Giverny or Chartres or explore shopping areas in Paris. On the Champs-Elysées, walk till evening and climb the Arc de Triomphe.

Day 7: Going on a bus "69" tour of Paris, then to Père Lachaise Cemetery, Montmartre, Sacré-Cœur or Jacquemart-André Museum, Marmottan Museum, and/or more shopping and café hopping.

Summer is typically hot and dry; take air-conditioning rooms if you cannot stand the hot weather. Look out for more vacancies in August, as some hotels may be offering discounts. Fewer deals are available during May, June, September, and October because hotel hunting can be challenging. In late spring and fall, the weather is best, and large crowds are attracted by them. The French close their businesses en masse in August, but tourists will hardly see any difference.

In addition, Paris makes an excellent winter destination too. The city has cheaper airfares during this time as well as cozy cafes that come alive without the throngs of tourists that visit during peak season. However, be prepared for freezing temperatures, including rain, so remember your jacket and umbrella. To keep warm, make sure you bring hats, gloves, scarves, umbrellas, and heavy shoes.

Before You Go

Ensure an Easy Journey by Following These Tips: To have a quiet vacation, ensure you always carry these items with you and do not lose them.

Verify Your Travel Documents: Make sure your passport is still valid. If it will expire within six months of your return date, then renew it now. Allow at least 6 weeks for passport processing. Verify what COVID entry requirements are in place, such as evidence of vaccination or negative test results.

Organize Transportation: Book your international flights and work out how to get around once you arrive. If you plan to travel outside Paris, research train reservations, rail passes, and car rentals.

Book Accommodations Early: Especially during peak season or major holidays and festivals, plan for lodgings.

Reserve Key Attractions: Some attractions require booking, including the Louvre, Sainte-Chapelle, Orangerie, and Versailles; pre-booking is also recommended for the Eiffel Tower, Catacombs, and Conciergerie.

Buy a Paris Museum Pass: Purchase the pass online beforehand if it matches your itinerary; use it to get timed entry slots at included sites.

Consider Travel Insurance: Weigh the cost of insurance against potential losses. Check whether your current health insurance or home/renters insurance covers overseas travel and belongings while abroad.

Tell Your Bank: Notifying your bank that you will be using debit or credit cards in Europe is important too. Find out about the transaction costs involved, plus request a contactless card that has a PIN if you don't have one. Euros can be withdrawn from ATMs in Europe, so there's no need to carry them along with you.

Smartphone Efficiency: Sign up for an international service plan to minimize costs or simply rely on Wi-Fi in Europe; Download the necessary apps like maps, translators, and transit schedules.

Pack Light: You'll be carrying your bags more than you imagine. Try to travel with only one carry-on bag and a daypack. Refer to the packing checklist in the Practicalities chapter as a reference guide.

Travel Smart: Adopting a positive attitude, arming yourself with good information (like this book), and planning to travel intelligently will lay the groundwork for success.

Keep Your Eyes Open: Real pickpockets can be found at crowded tourist sites. Regard sudden commotions as attempts at distracting you so that someone else can steal from you. Keep your cash, credit cards, and passport in a money belt beneath your clothes. Carry only a small amount of spending money, either in your front pocket or wallet.

Beating the Heat: If heat bothers you, choose an air-conditioned hotel, start sightseeing early in the morning, take time off around noon, and continue exploring late into the evening.

Stay Flexible: Build downtime into your schedule, such as for picnics, laundry days, people-watching, lingering dinners, or shopping trips; Embrace spontaneity and French warmth by allowing yourself some pleasant surprises.

Plunge In: Have a delightful picnic on the river bank, treat yourself to a long meal at a lovely bistro, or join locals for a game of friendly boules. I am so excited for you to find out why I love Paris so much when we visit my favorite haunts together.

"Have wonderful travels! Bon voyage!"

Before setting off, you should look up the most recent health and safety advice, which may include travel restrictions for your destination. Visit the US State Department's travel pages (www.travel.state.gov) and the Centers for Disease Control and Prevention's travel section (www.cdc.gov/travel) for updates.

Tourist Information: Paris' tourist information offices ("TI" in this guide; www.parisinfo.com) are great sources of information. They sell museum passes as well as individual attraction tickets, but at a small charge and with queues that can be longer than those at the museums themselves. They also issue local concert and event tickets. The main TI is located at Hôtel de Ville (open daily from 10:00 to 18:00, 29 Rue de Rivoli, on the north side). TIs in both airports have extended hours and are conveniently located.

Overcoming the Language Barrier: Many Parisians indeed speak English to some extent; however, it would be helpful to know simple terms such as bonjour (good day), pardon (excuse me), s'il vous plaît (please), merci/thank-you, and au revoir (goodbye). Begin each interaction with "Bonjour Madame or Monsieur" and end it with "Au revoir Madame or Monsieur."

Time Zones: France is six hours ahead of US East Coast Time and nine hours ahead of US West Coast Time. Get your phone's world clock app installed to have an easy time converter with you all the way.

Business Hours: Most smaller shops are open from Monday to Saturday (1000–1200 and 1400–1900), closing only on Sundays. However, big grocery stores like Galeries Lafayette near Opera Garnier, Carrousel du Louvre underground mall, and some stores near Sevres-Babylone, Champs-Elysées, and Marais operate every day. A lot of small markets, boulangeries (bakeries), and street markets close at noon on Sunday.

Electricity: Europe uses a 220-volt electrical system, while North America uses 110 volts. The majority of modern appliances and electronics (like laptops, phones, cameras, newer hair dryers, and CPAP machines) can accommodate this voltage automatically. Nevertheless, you will need a two-pin round adapter plug, which can be purchased easily from travel shops in the US.

Around Town

Bookstores: Shakespeare and Company (37 Rue de la Bûcherie, 75005 Paris, Mo St-Michel), open from 10 to 10 every day (+33 1 43 25 40 93).

Smith&Son (248 Rue de Rivoli, Paris, near the Tuileries, Mo Concorde), opens at 9 a.m. on weekdays and closes at 7 p.m. (Mon-Sat), while on Sundays they open at 12 p.m. and close at 7 p.m. (+33-1-44-77-88-99). Abbey Bookshop (closed Sundays) (29 Rue de la Parcheminerie between Blvd. St-Germain and Blvd. St-Michel in the Latin Quarter of Paris; phone +33(0)1-46-33-16-24, métro stop Cluny-LLa Sorbonne) San Francisco Book Company (17 rue Monsieur le Prince, across from Luxembourg Gardens—Métro Odéon), open Thursday–Tuesday from ten til noon, then on one side of the street closes doors till eight o'clock the next day when it will be closed (Wednesday is a holiday for this shop with telephone number +33(0)1-43-29-15-70). Laundry The concierge should be able to direct you to a self-service laundry or laundry service in your hotel.

Restrooms (WCs) Most museums have restrooms inside them that are accessible even if you have not paid admission. There are also public restrooms on many streets; some people might want to tip the attendant.

Tobacco stands (tabacs) Many tabacs sell metro tickets as well as local stamps such as "France" value and "tous pays." Usually, they would be found below a sign that reads "Tabac" and features a logo like a cylinder with a red background.

ARRIVAL IN PARIS

Charles De Gaulle Airport: The main airport in Paris has three terminals: T-1, T-2, and T-3. Most of the US flights land at either T-1 or T-2. All the terminals are linked by the CDGVAL shuttle train. It takes about an hour to change terminals. Paris Tourisme information desks, ATMs, Wi-Fi, shops, cafes, and bars can be found in both Terminals 1 and 2. The tax-refund centers for VAT refunds are located in the check-in area.

Traveling from Charles de Gaulle Airport to Paris is possible in several ways:

Taxi or Uber: Taxis have a flat rate to Paris (€60 to the Left Bank, €55 to the Right Bank for up to four passengers with luggage; extra charges apply for additional passengers). When returning to the airport from

Paris, call a taxi via your hotel. Nevertheless, due to bus-only lanes that cannot be used by Uber vehicles, expect it to take quite a while longer than when using taxis. In CDG, there is no specific place where ride-sharing pickup occurs, which means you have to plan where you will meet your driver.

RoissyBus: This bus stops near Opéra Métro station in central Paris (€15, runs from 6:00 till 23:00 every day of the week, and goes every 50 minutes approximately; tickets can be bought at the ticket machine at the airport's desk; the Paris tourist office is also available on the bus). Once in Opéra, you can go anywhere in town via subway or a €15 cab fare.

Suburban Train: The fastest public transport into downtown is RER/Train-B (11.50 euros), departing every half hour between 5:00 a.m. and midnight each day of the week, with a trip taking about thirty-five minutes on average (though some trains may take longer, probably forty-five minutes). At CDG, there are two RER-B stations: one is located at Terminal 2, and a less busy one is next to Terminal 3 (Roissypole). These stations are connected by the CDGVAL shuttle to all terminals. The RER/Train-B goes to Gare du Nord, Châtelet-Les Halles, St. Michel, and Luxembourg with easy subway connections. To get to RER/Train-B from any terminal, follow the train signs (from T-1, take the CDGVAL shuttle to T-3/Roissypole).

Some Important Details

Rumors have it that the French are unfriendly and reluctant to speak English. In my opinion, French people are just as nice as anybody else (though slightly more formal), and a lot of Parisians speak English quite well. But it is important to **keep your expectations realistic**: French waiters are hired to be efficient, not conversational.

Parisians might appear disinterested, but most times they're only observing good manners and traditions. From their view, always-smiling Americans can seem friendly but insincere.

The best advice? Slow down. Embrace the pace of life here in France. Impatient tourists who fail to see the beauty of watching people pass by from a sunny café often misunderstand the attitudes of French citizens. These hosts have enough holiday time and work only 35 hours per week, so they cannot understand why you should hurry when taking advantage of leisure moments or holidays. By appreciating the culture of France, it would make your experience more fulfilling.

Other Arrival Points

Orly Airport: This convenient airport may seem small but has everything that is needed, including Paris Tourisme counters inside the arrivals zone where you can purchase Paris Museum Passes as well as public transport tickets into the town itself. There are several ways to get into Paris, which include taking a taxi (€32 to get to Left Bank or €37 to Right Bank), using the Uber app, or using the Orlybus to go directly on RER/Train-B, allowing access at locations such as Luxembourg Garden, Notre-Dame, Châtelet's handy metro line 1, and Gare du Nord.

Paris Train Stations: There are six main train stations in Paris serving different regions. For example, Gare du Nord is an arrival point for Eurostar from London. The most comprehensive train schedules can be found on Bahn.com, while Sncf.com provides information regarding domestic travel; tickets should be bought at En Oui Sncf/en. Pre-book high-speed TGV trains (also called "InOui"). To see if a rail pass will save you money.

Getting around Paris

Paris is such a compact city that you are never more than a 10-minute walk from a Metro station and buses are plentiful. For more details on Paris' public transport, please see Ratp.fr. To get to know it, however, refer to the fold-out Metro map at the back of this book; buy a Navigo Easy Card; and learn some key bus lines for easy orientation around the city.

Ticket Purchase: Here are your options for travel by metro, public buses, and RER/suburban trains. In most cases, tourists would find the Navigo Easy Card as their easiest choice (€2 re-loadable). You can load funds onto your Navigo Easy card and top up per ride (€1.90/ride) or purchase a 10-ride pass (Navigo avec un carnet, €14.90, Zones 1-2) or daily pass (Navigo Jour, €7.50, Zones 1-2). Extra zones may be added to your day pass (€12.40; Zones 1-4 cover areas like Versailles). Buy your Navigo Easy or Découverte card at any staffed Métro station or a tabac; all stations have machines for reloading a Navigo Easy Card, plus there is also an option to download a digital one on the RATP app, where you can use your smartphone to enter the Métro or you can board a bus. See Ratp.fr for details.

By Metro: From 5:30 AM until midnight, with additional hourly service on Fridays and Saturdays until after midnight, Europe's best subway system runs every day. Locate the nearest Metro stop from where you are coming from or going, then check which other lines it connects with. Lines are both color-coded and numbered, named after the stops they go through in order of termination. Signs in the station will guide you towards where you need to be to catch the right train (e.g., direction: La Défense). At the turnstile, touch your Navigo card on the purple pad, wait for a green validation light and a "ding" sound, and then pass through.

Be prepared to walk long distances within Metro stations. To change lines, follow signs marked correspondence (connection). Once you arrive at your destination, the blue and white Sortie (exit) signs will help guide you. Use neighborhood maps to decide which exit is best.

Metro resources: Metro maps are also included in this book and can be found as free handouts in stations, online at Ratp.fr, or on free Paris maps available at your hotel. Take extra care, especially when buying tickets, passing through turnstiles, or getting on or off crowded trains, because thieves like operating in such places.

By RER/Suburban Train The RER: Suburban train operates like the Métro but has different rates for travel outside Paris, such as Versailles, that usually cost more than an ordinary ticket within city limits. Traditionally called RER, it's also known simply as "Train." These routes are shown by thick lines on subway maps and labeled with letters A–K. Unlike Metro, not all RER trains stop at every station, so check the above platform sign or screen to see if your stop is there.

City Bus: Most stops have city bus maps, schedules, live arrival displays, and a neighborhood map; some even provide mobile phone chargers. Buses accept Navigo cards just like the Metro and RER do. Remember to purchase your card before you get on board (available at Metro stations and Tabacs). From one bus journey to another within 1½ hours of hopping onto a bus line, holders of Navigo Easy Card However, passengers cannot change buses between Métro/suburban rails or make multiple trips on one bus fare (in such cases, you need another fare).

Place your Navigo card on the purple touchpad. Keep track of upcoming stops on the display inside. When you're ready to leave, press the red emergency button to stop at the next station and go out through the center door or the one in the back. Avoid peak hours (Mon-Fri 8:00–9:30 and 17:30–19:30), when you can get somewhere by taking a subway.

Useful bus lines include no. 69, which runs from Rue Cler past Quai d'Orsay and across Ile St-Louis and le Marais to Père Lachaise Cemetery or vice versa, and scenic bus no. 73, which runs from Musée d'Orsay up the Champs-Elysées to l'Arc de Triomphe. Check with your hotel's receptionist for a convenient nearby bus stop that would fit into your sightseeing plans.

By Uber: In Paris, Uber works somewhat as it does everywhere else and is generally more enjoyable than traditional cabs are known for being. The drivers usually seem friendlier and more flexible, but their prices are still comparable with those of taxis. In case you cannot find a taxi stand or identify a taxi driver's car within five minutes, you can request an Uber ride via text message. However, during rush hour, it is better off with taxes; they make use of bus lanes while Uber cars get fixed in traffic jams, especially when one wants to travel from Paris' airports to its center, owing to having flat rates and set pick-up points versus the dynamic pricing system used by Uber, which requires users to specify where they will be picked up before getting there.

By Taxi: Parisian taxis are an affordable option, especially when traveling with another person or family members. Fares (including supplementary charges posted in English on back windows) are simple and regulated strictly by law. A maximum of four people can be taken in any taxi, although some drivers may not want to do that. Larger groups are advised to pre-book a larger taxi.

The meter starts at €2.60, and the minimum charge is €7.30. For example, a 20-minute ride (such as from the Bastille to the Eiffel Tower) costs around €25. Also, taxis charge more during rush hours, nighttime, all day on Sunday, and for additional passengers. When it comes to tipping, always round up to the nearest euro (at least €0.50).

To get a taxi, you can stand on the sidewalk with your arm extended or look out for the circled "T" symbol of a cab stand on good city maps and many maps in this book. To order a taxi in English, call G7 Cab Company (+33 1 41 27 66 99) or ask your hotel or restaurant staff; immediate orders cost a fixed fee of €4 while booking ahead is charged €7. It may be difficult to find a taxi during evening peak periods or if it rains, late at weekends, and after Metro closure times, though early morning trains or flights require pre-booking by making arrangements through your hotel.

By Bike: It is really easy to ride a bike in Paris. It is located on flat land, with over 370 miles of bicycle paths and access to many bus and taxi lanes that have priority (exercise caution while using this lane).

Paris.fr provides neighborhood bike path maps. Paris Tourist Information (TI) centers offer a useful map called "Paris a Vélo" showing all dedicated bike paths. Different versions are also available at newsstands, some bookstores, and department stores.

Hôtel de Ville has Bike About Tours, where you can rent bikes for €20/day or €17. Rue du Pont Louis Philippe (see map, Mo: St-Paul), while Fat Tire Tours has them near the Eiffel Tower at €4/hour or 24 Rue Edgar Faure, Mo: Dupleix or La Motte-Picquet-Grenelle. Both companies also organize great biking tours. Thousands of Vélib bikes are distributed around town through the city's Vélib program (from vélo + libre = "bike freedom") that serves locals as well as tourists. This is good for one-way trips or rentals lasting a few hours. Also, Lime Bikes offers bike rentals and e-scooters through an easy-to-use app (www.li.me).

Money

France uses the euro: 1 euro (€) = about $1.10. For example, to change euros into dollars, you add roughly 10% to the amount: €10 = about $11; €50 = about $55. You may find www.oanda.com useful in checking for current exchange rates. Here are my ideas on how I would go about wise money management while in Europe.

For most purchases, big (hotels and advance tickets) and small (shops or food stands), use your credit card. The commonest and easiest cards to employ are termed "tap-to-pay" or "contactless." Be sure that you have a tap-to-pay credit card (look for the 'tap-to-pay symbol"—four squiggly lines). Always know your numeric PINs for all of your debit and credit cards, which consist of four digits each. Should you not possess one, ask for it since there are instances where it may be required, such as when making some payments.

Use an ATM (distributeur), and a small amount of local currency can be withdrawn using a debit card. While most transactions occur via card, cash can still come in handy if your card malfunctions, or perhaps for tips or local guides. Keep your money belt containing cards and cash safe.

Sometimes self-service payment machines like transit-ticket kiosks do not accept US cards. Then there is an attendant who will take this no-problem or otherwise pay with cash. Trade dealings involving credit.

Cards and Debit Cards

You could therefore rely on your credit card when it comes to large expenses such as hotels together with bookings as well as petty acquisitions such as little stores besides food markets; this is because they accept plastic money just like any other place in France does with ease through contactless smart systems. Get an insight into what contactless payments involve. Confirm whether yours has a tap-to-pay feature (look for four squiggly lines) or if you can get one that does. Make sure that you know the four-digit PINs of your debit and credit cards in case they are needed during a purchase.

To withdraw some local currency, use your debit card at an ATM (distributeur). Most transactions are done through cards, but having some cash can be handy if your card stops working or for tipping and paying local guides. Keep all your money, as well as your bank cards, in a money belt.

Self-service payment machines (e.g., for transit tickets) may not always accept US plastic. In such cases, look up who would qualify to process your card by hand or give them cash.

Tipping in France: It is customary but less generous in terms of tipping (donner un pourboire) as it is practiced in the United States. However, there are some general pointers here.

Restaurants: For example, cafes and restaurants usually include a 12–15% service charge on their menu prices. You should not tip, but an extra 5% is a nice thank you for exceptional service. Be prepared to offer tips with cash when using credit cards.

Taxis: Pay an amount that rounds up the fare for an average taxi ride (for example, if the fare comes out to €13, pay €14).

Services: Generally speaking, someone in tourism or services doing outstanding work will get a Euro or two from me because of the exceptional effort he or she has put into making it great. However, if I am unsure whether or not certain workers require tips, I usually ask locals about it first before getting embarrassed over something petty that could ruin my vacation.

Staying Connected

Making International Calls

From a Mobile Phone: The phone numbers listed in this guide are meant to be dialed from a US mobile phone. To make an international call, hold the 0 key until it becomes a plus sign, then type in the country code (33 for France), and finally enter the phone number.

From a US Landline to Europe: Substitute the plus (+) symbol with 011 (the United States/Canada international access code), but dial the country code (33 for France) as well as the phone number.

From a European Landline to the US or Europe: Instead of the + sign, insert 00, which is a European international access code; then dial the country code (33 for France, 1 for the USA); and finally, your destination number. For additional support on how to call abroad, check out HowToCallAbroad.com.

Using Your Phone in Europe

Register for an International Plan: Return connected economically by selecting an international plan through your carrier. Most companies have bundles that include talk time, texts, and data.

Look out for free Wi-Fi: Unless you have unlimited data, use Wi-Fi whenever you can access the internet. Many hotels in Europe provide free wireless connectivity, while other cafes offer hotspots for their customers' use. Other areas where Wi-Fi can be used include tourist information centers, public squares, major museums, transit hubs, airports, and trains and buses.

Minimize cellular network usage: Even with a global data plan that will work worldwide, save data by not sending photos or videos when using Skype, FaceTime, or other media streaming services, especially if it is not connected to Wifi. Download maps offline so that they won't consume your data.

Buy eSim: You can download from the App Store or Google Play, apps like **Airalo** or **Holafly**. These applications allow you to "virtually" purchase a local SIM. You can choose the rate plan based on your days of stay or how many gigabytes of Internet traffic you need.

Immerse yourself in the allure of Paris with my expertly curated insights, blending the charm of a native Parisian with the practical advice of a seasoned traveler who calls both Paris and the USA home."

Packing Checklist

Clothing:

- 5 shirts (long- & short-sleeve)

- 2 pairs of pants (or skirts/capris)

- 1 pair of shorts

- 5 pairs of underwear and socks

- 1 pair of walking shoes

- Sweater or warm layer

- Rainproof jacket with hood

- Tie, scarf, belt, and/or hat

- Swimsuit

- Sleepwear/loungewear

Money:

- Debit card(s)

- Credit card(s)

- Hard cash recommended (US $100-200)
- Money belt

Documents:

- Passport
- Other required ID: vaccine card/Covid test, entry visa, etc.
- Driver's license, student ID, hostel card, etc.
- Tickets & confirmations: flights, hotels, trains, rail pass, car rental, sight entries
- Insurance details
- Guidebooks & maps
- Notepad & pen
- Journal

- **Toiletries**:
- Soap, shampoo, toothbrush, toothpaste, floss, deodorant, sunscreen, brush etc.

Medicines & Vitamins

- First-aid kit
- Glasses/contacts/sunglasses
- Face masks & hand sanitizer

- Mag citrate

Sewing Kit:

- Small sewing kit
- Tissue packet (for restrooms)
- Earplugs

Electronics:

- Mobile phone
- Camera and accessories
- Headphones/earbuds
- Chargers and batteries
- Plug adapters

Learn some Phrases in French

French Pronunciation

I've provided an approximate guide to pronouncing each phrase in this post using phonetic English. While this can't replace listening to recordings or native speakers, it will help you get started. The letter 'j' represents the French 'j' sound, which is softer than the English 'j' in 'John'.

For an in-depth look at pronunciation, check out my detailed French pronunciation guide.

A Note on Tu and Vous

French, like many other languages, differentiates between "you" based on familiarity.

The basic rule is:

- Use **vous** when speaking to strangers, especially those older than you.

- Use **tu** when speaking to someone you know well or to children.

In my list, I've provided the most appropriate form for each phrase. Where both forms might be needed, I've included both.

In very casual spoken French, **tu es** and **tu** can be shortened to **t'es** and **t'as**.

"This might not be strictly correct, but it's very common.". I've included this form for some informal expressions to illustrate where you might encounter it.

If you're interested in more informal language, check out my post on 23 colloquial French phrases to impress the locals.

Basic French Greetings

Let's start with some fundamental French greetings. These are quite straightforward, and you probably already know a few of them.

Bonjour! – Hello! (the standard greeting in French)
(Bon jour)

Bonsoir! – Good evening! (used instead of bonjour in the evening)
(Bon swah)

Salut! – Hi! (a more casual greeting)
(sa loo)

Enchanté(e)! – Nice to meet you! (commonly used when meeting someone for the first time)
(on shon tay)

Common French Phrases to Continue a Conversation

After greeting someone, you'll likely want to engage in some small talk. Here are a few standard questions and responses:

Ça va? – How are you? (the basic way to ask how someone is)
(sa va)

Ça roule? – How's it going? (a much more casual way to ask the same question, perfect for close friends)
(sa rule)

Comment vas-tu/comment tu vas? Comment allez-vous? – How are you? (a slightly more formal version of ça va? in both informal and formal forms)
(Komon va too, Komon tallay voo) – the 'n' is nasal and do not pronounced strongly

Ça va/Je vais bien – I'm well (the first version remains unchanged. as the question but with a different intonation; the second is another way to say it)
(sa va/juh vay byan)

Et toi? – And you?
(ay twah)

Essential French Phrases for Politeness

Here are some fundamental expressions of courtesy that you should know from the start.

Merci – Thank you (the standard word)
(mair see)

Merci bien – Thank you (adds extra politeness or friendliness)
(mair see byan)

Merci beaucoup – Thank you very much (expressing more gratitude)
(mair see bo coo)

De rien – It's nothing (the usual reply to Merci)
(duh ryan)

Excusez-moi / pardon – Means Excuse me, sorry (both are used to apologize or when trying to pass by)
(eh skyoo zay mwah/pah don)

Excusez-moi?/Comment ? – Sorry? Excuse me? Pardon? (used when you don't hear what someone says. Note that the French word "pardon" shouldn't be used for this)
(eh skyoo zay mwah/komon)

Je suis désolé(e) – I'm sorry (a stronger apology than "excusez-moi" or "pardon")
(juh swee dehsolay)

Vas-y, Allez-y – Go on, go ahead (telling someone to move forward or to help themselves)
(va zee, allay zee, sair twah)

Essential French Phrases for Dealing with Problems

Here are some important phrases for dealing with problems or when things aren't going as planned.

Pouvez-vous…? – Can you…? (can be combined with various verbs)
(poo vay voo)

Pouvez-vous le répéter s'il vous plaît? – Can you repeat it please?
(poo vay voo luh reh peh tay sih voo play)

Pouvez-vous m'aider s'il vous plaît? – Can you help me please?
(poo vay voo mayday sih voo play)

Je ne comprends pas – I don't understand
(juh nuh compron pah)

Je n'ai rien compris! – I didn't understand anything/I haven't
understood anything (juh nay rien compree)

Je ne parle pas (beaucoup) français – I don't speak (much) French
(juh nuh pahl pah bo coo duh fron say)

Je suis perdu – I'm lost
(juh swee pair doo)

Qu'est-ce que ça veut dire? – What does that mean?
(kess kuh sa vuh deer)

Parlez-vous français/anglais? – Do you speak French/English?
(parlay voo fron say/ong glay)

Je ne me sens pas très bien – I don't feel very well.
(juh nuh muh son pah tray byan)

Je suis malade – I'm ill/sick.
(juh swee ma lad)

Attention! Fais/faites attention! – Careful! Be careful!
(ah ton sion, fay/fet ah ton sion)

Au secours! – Help!
(oh suhcoor)

French Question Words

Learning basic question words can help you a lot, even if you don't know much else. Here they are in French:

Quoi? – What?
(kwah)

Quand? – When? (kon)

Qui? – Who? (kee)

Comment? – How? (komon)

Combien? – How many? (kom byan)

Où? – Where? (oo)

Pourquoi? – Why? (pour kwah)

Quel(le)? – Which? (this question and thath word agrees with the noun. The four possible forms are quel, quelle, quells.
(kell)

Common French Questions

Now that you know the essential question words, here are some common French questions you might ask or be asked.

Comment tu t'appelles? Tu t'appelles comment? – What's your name? (the first is more formal; the second is common in spoken French)
(komon too tappel, too tappel komon)

Quel âge as-tu? T'as quel âge? – How old are you? (first version is formal; the second is more common in informal French)
(kel aj ah too, too ah kel aj)

Quelle heure est-il? Il est quelle heure? – What's the time? (both forms are possible; second is more common in informal French)
(kel er et ill/ill ay kell er)

C'est combien? Ça coûte combien? – How much is it? How much does that cost?
(say kom byan - sa coot kom byan)

Tu viens d'où? T'es d'où? – Where do you come from? / Where are you from?
(too vyen doo/tay doo)

Tu comprends? – Do you understand? (ask by changing intonation)
(too kom pron)

Tu parles anglais/français? – Do you speak English/French? (informal, spoken version; ask by changing intonation)
(too pahl ong glai/fron say)

Parlez-vous anglais/français? – Do you speak English/French? (formal, polite version)
(parlay voo ong glai/ fron say)

Où est la salle de bains? Or Où sont les toilettes ? – Where is the toilet?
(oo ay lah sal duh ban or oo son lay twah let)

Important Answers in French

Here are some essential expressions for sharing information about yourself and answering basic questions in French.

Je m'appelle... – My name is... (the standard expression)

(juh mappel)

Je suis (Roger/Irlandais(e)/professeur) – I'm Roger/Irish/a teacher (used for your name, nationality, job, and more)

(juh swee roh jay/ear lon day/ear lon days/pro feh Suhr)

J'ai 30 ans – I'm 30 (literally, "I have 30 years" – remember to include "ans" at the end) (jay tront on)

Oui – Yes (wee)

Non – No (noh)

Peut-être – Maybe (puh tetr)

Tout le temps or tous les jours – All the time or every day

(too luh ton/too lay jour)

Parfois, des fois – Sometimes

(pah fwah, day fwah)

Jamais – Never (ja may)

Bien sûr – Of course

(byan sure – pronounced with an 's' sound, not 'sh')

Simple French Phrases for Special Occasions

If you're lucky enough to make French friends, you might be invited to special occasions. Here are the phrases you'll need:

Amuse-toi bien! Amusez-vous bien! – Have fun! (ah my twah byan, ah myoozay voo byan)

Bon voyage! – Have a good trip! (Bon voyaj)

Bonnes vacances! – Have a good holiday! (Bonn vah konce)

Bon appétit! – Bon appétit! (the final 't' is not pronounced in French) (Bon appuh tee)

Félicitations! – Congratulations! (fay liss ee tah sion)

Bienvenue! – Welcome! (byan vuh noo)

Joyeux anniversaire! – Happy birthday! (jway uh zannee ver sair)

Joyeux Noël! – Merry Christmas! (jway uh no ell)

Bonne année! – Happy New Year! (Bonn annay)

Essential French Expressions for Saying Goodbye

Au revoir! – Goodbye! (the standard phrase) (oh ruh vwah)

Bonne journée! – Good day! (used at the end of a conversation) (bonn jour nay)

Bonne soirée! – Good evening! (feminine form of bonsoir) (bonn swah ray)

Bonne nuit! – Good night! (bonn nwee)

À bientôt! – See you soon! (ah byan toe)

À demain! – See you tomorrow! (ah duh man)

GET YOUR FREE BONUS NOW!

Download for free with the below instruction!

Scan the Qr Code below and Unlock your BONUS about
Paris and elevate your knowledge of France

A WALK IN PARIS

For a long time now, Paris has been considered the center of Europe's culture. We'll kick off our tour from the historical island of Ile de la Cité and cross on to the Left Bank through 80 generations of history. From a Celtic fishing village to a Roman metropolis, from Medieval capital to cradle of Revolution, and from bohemian cafes in the 1920s to today's dynamic modern-day Paris. On this trail, you will be able to see two of Paris' most famous landmarks: Notre Dame and Sainte-Chapelle. The process there involves some modifications due to renovation works at Notre Dame following a destructive fire in 2019.

The walk is approximately three miles long and may last about four hours, allowing for exploration of sights. Give yourself some extra time for a nice lunch, café crème, antiquarian bookstores, or watching the Seine river flow peacefully.

Paris Passlib': Several destinations on this route are included in the Paris Passlib', which offers good value for money and saves time (see Landmarks). Get your pass at Ile de la Cité, newsstand/gift shop (5 Boulevard du Palais), opposite the Sainte-Chapelle entrance.

Notre-Dame Cathedral: The cathedral can only be accessed from the outside because, after it caught fire in 2019, its interior was destroyed completely. The internal works and tower stairs will continue until complete reopening in December 2024. For the best view of the church facade (and also the stained-glass windows at Ste Chapelle), don't forget your binoculars.

Sainte-Chapelle: €11.50 timed entry, €18.50 joint ticket with Conciergerie, included in Museum Pass, reserve online (limited on-site tickets), open 9 a.m.–7 p.m. daily (5 p.m. closure October–March); €3 audio guide, 4 Boulevard du Palais, Mo: Cité, +33 1 53 40 60 80, www.sainte-chapelle.fr.

Deportation Memorial: Complimentary, open 10 a.m.–7 p.m. daily (5 p.m. closure October–March), occasional unexpected closures, a free 45-minute audio guide, and tours are available. Mo: Cité, +33 6 14 67 54 98.

Conciergerie: €11.50 timed entry, €18.50 joint ticket with Sainte-Chapelle, included in Museum Pass, book online, open 9:30 a.m.–6 p.m. daily, multimedia guide €5, 2 Boulevard du Palais, Mo: Cité, +33 (0)1.53.40.60.80, www.paris-conciergerie.fr.

Beat the rush: This district is most packed mid-morning to mid-afternoon, especially Tuesdays (Louvre closure) and weekends. Get there early or stay longer at the end of your day; Sainte-Chapelle's small size sometimes causes lines. Security lines are shortest in the early morning, though she did not tell me that this was a drawback of staying up late or getting up early.

The Walk Begins

Beginning Point: Notre-Dame Cathedral The first place you will see Notre-Dame Cathedral is an island on the Seine River, which is considered the most important Paris center point. The nearest Metro stations are Cité, Hôtel de Ville, and St. Michel.

Notre Dame and Its Vicinity Look at this wonderful view from the cathedral, Place du Parvis, and the city around it with its abundance of people and international tourists. You are in the middle of France geographically. Every measurement for distance in France comes from a small bronze plaque known as "Point Zero" (it can be found inside a 30-yard span lying right ahead of the cathedral). It has also been referred to as being symbolic because this place is situated right at the heart of France. Think about how much history must have happened right here.

Notre Dame Throughout History

Those who come after us will recall that it was on April 15th, 2019 when flames destroyed Notre Dame Cathedral. This tragic incident marks only one page in Paris' long and dramatic history.

Imagine how this site has evolved over thousands of years. In ancient days, some 2,300 years ago, just a few inhabitants lived here; they were called "Parisii." They fished and traded by crossing the river at that spot. Following their conquest of the Parisii tribe by force, the Romans built their temple to Jupiter on what is present-day "Notre Dame" (52 BC). A new Christian church replaced it when the Franks invaded Rome and changed its name to St. Etienne. By 800 AD or so, Charlemagne, whose statue is located near its right side, the Frankish king had begun reshaping what would become modern France.

By 1200 AD, there must have been construction workers all around transforming ruins into an old brickwork church, which we now call Notre Dame. Eventually, we got a pointy spire and two half-finished steeples at the front, which we still see today as short bell towers.

By 1800 AD, it was a ruined old building stripped of its central spire to safeguard people, and numerous statues on the facade were broken off during the Revolution. The square outside was crowded with medieval houses, including Notre Dame's bell towers. That was what inspired Victor Hugo's story about a deformed hunchback spying from above Paris. His book became so popular that it led to public support for restoring the cathedral.

In 1844 AD, young architect Eugène-Emmanuel Viollet-le-Duc completed a major Neo-Gothic renovation. There, he fixed new 300-foot spires and added more sculptures, some of which were grotesque monsters.

After eight centuries, Notre Dame had become the world's most famous Gothic masterpiece. This was the cathedral that stood when the 2019 fire occurred, marking the start of yet another chapter in Paris's history.

There are many remnants of ancient Paris under the square around Notre-Dame Cathedral, but most of it is unexcavated. The archeological Crypt you can see on your right side has some objects retrieved from beneath these streets (for details, refer to Sights). Now let us turn our attention to the stunning Notre-Dame Cathedral.

The Notre-Dame Front

Notre-Dame structure remains largely untouched by a devastating fire in 2019. We will look at all affected parts later, but for now, let us just concentrate on this beautiful remaining front part.

This is a massive church dedicated to "Our Lady" (Notre Dame), with the statue of the Virgin Mary holding baby Jesus within the halo formed by a rose window. Nevertheless, this cathedral, which looks so grand, has always had a symbolic meaning of mercy and love for all the Christians who worshiped there.

On the wall directly above or slightly beyond two-thirds up the left tower of Notre Dame is Paris' most photographed gargoyle. Step closer to the cathedral (as much as construction barriers allow) and examine statues decorating the left doorways.

St. Denis: On one side of this doorway, there is an image of St. Denis holding his head in his hands; he was beheaded by Roman pagans who wanted to discourage other people from converting to Christianity. However, early Christians were not easily discouraged because Denis took off his cut-off head he washed in fountain water before setting off to find a place where he could rest. A church replaced the old pagan temple once Christianity was firmly established.

Just come closer to this main entrance. Carved into stone above it are scenes from The Last Judgment.

Central Portal: Shown here is how everything will cease these days are ending. Christ is on his throne of judgment (just under arches with both hands raised). Underneath him, an angel and a devil's scales weigh souls, although this demon cheats by pressing down. Life's good guys stand on the left, looking up towards heaven, while the bad guys on the right are chained together and led away for a lengthy trip around the Louvre on the hottest day in summer.

Go higher, still above the doorway arches, till you see a row of 28...

The Kings of Judah: During the French Revolution (1789–1799), they were mistaken for hated French monarchs, thereby symbolizing oppressive Catholicism associated with Notre Dame at that time. Revolutionaries stormed into the church shouting "Off with their heads!" and hacked off these statues' heads with glee. For so many years, there was a line of headless figures. The story does not end there; a schoolteacher buried these heads in his backyard, and they were discovered by accident in 1977. Today, the original heads can be seen at the Cluny Museum, which is just a short walk away (see Sights).

Do not forget that for close to a millennium, Notre Dame has been more than just an attractive site for tourists but also a church. Drown yourself in the image of this cathedral in its full glory. In case you can't enter this place today, figuratively take off your hat and read on.

Virtual Tour of Notre-Dame's Interior

Make sure your device supports embedded audio if you would like to hear the audio tours.

"Enter" the church as a simple peasant used to do before to form the "Notre Dame Interior" map. Imagine yourself stepping into dim earthly caverns lit up only by rays of light from colored glass windows, along with their ethereal quality. The priest's Mass echoes through the hall as your eyes follow the slender columns up ten stories to the ceiling's praying-hands arches. Walk directly down the central nave, flanked by two aisles of columns. The entire area could hold about 10,000 worshippers.

Having reached the altar, you are now in the center of this cruciform cathedral, where Christians take Holy Communion. This place has been sacred to Romans, Christians, and even atheists at times. The French Revolution saw the church stripped of all its religious symbols, and mannequins were put at the altar dressed as Lady Liberty.

Suppose you took a walk around this cathedral; you'd realize that it is a Parisian treasure house for the Smithsonian Institution. For instance, there's a revered Crown of Thorns that legend says Jesus wore (Stored safely away in the Treasury). There's a gold-and-enamel casket dedicated to St. Geneviève (fifth century), Paris' patron saint who saved her city from Attila the Hun by praying. There is a painting dedicated to Thomas Aquinas, a philosopher-priest (1225–1274) who studied at the University of Paris while sketching some influential theological works he shaped on faith and reason. A tall statue of Joan of Arc stands out. They rallied her nation to chase away English intruders from Paris. (This former "witch" was eventually canonized— right here in Notre Dame—despite being burned at the stake.)

The oldest part of the church is the north transept, which has a blue-and-purple rose window. It still has its original medieval glass, but it is currently obscured. The newest addition is the massive white tarp covering the roof during renovation. End your virtual tour at one of several chapels where believers can reflect on and light (in their minds) a candle, hoping that one day the interior will shine again as before.

Let's walk down.

Rue du Cloître Notre-Dame

When you get to the back of the church, there are displays in English describing how the fire started and what followed after that, a rooster rescued from atop the steeple, and ongoing restoration efforts. You also have the opportunity to view this building up close. Note gaps in stained glass windows—each piece is being tested for lead levels necessary for worker safety as it undergoes restoration. See flying buttresses currently supported by timber frames.

Keep on walking away from us and figure out another iconic view of Notre Dame later across the river. After the cathedral garden, take some time to stop at...

Ile St. Louis

If Ile de la Cité is a history-laden tugboat, it's dragging this graceful residential rowboat full of posh lofts, stores, cozy restaurants, and famous ice cream parlors. Consider taking a brief detour via Pont St. Louis to explore this island (or return in the evening).

We will go towards Left Bank now. Walk with Notre Dame behind you to the south side; enter into a small grassy park on your left (behind a high green hedge).

Deportation Memorial

This memorial throws visitors into the horror suffered by 2,000 French victims of Nazi concentration camps [1940–1945]. Nazi Germany swiftly conquered France while Paris lived through war years under Nazi rule. Jewish people, as well as dissenters, were arrested and deported; many never returned.

As you go down the stairs, the city disappears. You become a prisoner, surrounded by walls. There are 20.0000 luminous crystals representing each of the lives lost in France. At one end of it flickers an eternal flame of hope. Written above the exit is a slogan borrowed from other Holocaust sites that says, "Forgive, but never forget."

Go back to the street level. Leave this garden and turn left, then cross over Pont de l'Archevêché. On getting to the Left Bank, move right along its bank and follow Notre Dame's south side. Now we will focus on nearby areas, around...

Left Bank

The Rive Gauche, or Seine's Left Bank—"left" if you were drifting downstream—retains many winding alleys and narrow structures from medieval times. The Right Bank near the Seine is more contemporary and business-centric, with broad avenues and harried Parisians in suits.

Here along the riverbank, pre-owned books are "big business" that are sold on stalls made of green metal at its parapet (bouquinistes). These people who sell literature take pride in being so laid-back. Operating since the mid-1500s, they have flexible hours and minimal overheads.

Directly across from Notre Dame is a gap in the stalls which leads to stairs descending to the river – ideal for getting away from crowds and...

Notre-Dame Side View

From this angle, both the cathedral's architecture and destruction by fire can be seen well. Previously it was topped by a green lead roof with Viollet-le-Duc's 300-foot spire; there were also several statues lining its base. All those are now gone as well as the lead roof plus all other windows except three huge rose windows (now covered). However, the church has survived incredibly long given that it was constructed during the Middle Ages. Its revolutionary innovation is now called the Gothic style.

Many Gothic features are noticeable at first glance: Pointed arches; delicate stone tracery defining window openings; pinnacles, rooftop statuary, and pointed spires covered with Holy Spirit flames (Flamboyant Gothic); plus flying buttresses—most impressive among them. These fifty-foot-long "beams" of stone sticking out from the church were vital elements of complex Gothic structures. The weight of a roof inside is directed outward through pointed arches rather than downward. "Flying" buttresses do this by pushing inward themselves. This interplay of forces enabled the Gothic architects to build higher churches with stained glass windows. From here, the Gothic style quickly spread throughout Paris and beyond. The wood scaffolds supporting flying buttresses are evidence of how they were raised.

Imagine Quasimodo (the fictional hunchback) hobbling across the roof among the "gargoyles." Grotesque figures jutting out from pillars or buttresses represent souls caught between heaven and earth. They also serve as rainspouts (sharing a French root with "gargle") when there are no evil spirits to fight.

Once more having reached the river, at Notre Dame in front of it is a bridge called "Pont au Double." Go upstairs, make a left turn on the crossing street and you will find Square Viviani. Pass by a famous tree nicknamed Robinier, an acacia planted in 1602; cross over it through that square; beyond it lays St. Julien-le-Pauvre – a tiny church made of rough stone. Leave this park passing a church on its other side into tiny Rue Galande.

A Gothic church is built by thirteen tourists: one spire, six columns, and six buttresses.

Paris in the Middle Ages

Twenty years after St. Julien-le-Pauvre was built, imagine Paris of about 1250. Walk a few steps around the church to see what it's like outside. The industrial and commercial boom that turned Paris into a vibrant metropolis had already begun; Notre Dame was almost complete, Sainte Chapelle had just been opened, and human knowledge was broadening as more students thronged the university's classes. The district around the church up to Rue Galande can still give you an idea of what medieval life was with its lean-to constructions and crooked old houses that have survived from those times. People clung together and made their homes anyhow they wanted to secure this central spot near the Seine—a principal trading road in those days. In this thickly populated region, however, there were other odors too—the smell of fish mixed with that of people living around you on every side. Return towards the river and turn left at Rue de la Bûcherie…

Shakespeare and Company Bookshop

The Left Bank has always been home to philosophers, thinkers, and poets since the medieval period besides butchers' shops and fish markets here. An idiosyncratic library continues the literary tradition from the original shop established in the 1920s on Rue de l'Odéon by Sylvia Beach – an American lover of intellectual emancipation who targeted America's post-War One Lost Generation individuals seeking self-improvement abroad through France.

America's affordable rents attracted writers fleeing prohibitionist America making them come to Paris where they would find abundant alcohol despite being conservative back home hence Sylvia Beach came up with the Shakespeare and Company bookshop, which became famous as a meeting point for renowned authors such as James Joyce, Ernest Hemingway, and Gertrude Stein, among others. Continue straight ahead onto Rue du Petit-Pont. Turn right into this fast north-south route (which becomes Rue St. Jacques) to the south, which was the Romans' main road 2000 years ago with chariots speeding in and out of the city. Make a right at St. Séverin Church, an excellent example of Gothic architecture, and enter the Latin Quarter.

Conciergerie

Once inside, you will see that this prison is very plain; however, it has great historical importance. The last queen consort of France in the ancient régime, Marie Antoinette, was held as a prisoner here till her execution.

Get a free map at reception, then follow this marked itinerary from room to room. Start at Room 1: the Large Salle de Gens d'Armes has low ceilings because it used to be a guardroom where guards had their meals. Proceed to the slightly raised area across from one side of this room (Room 4—now converted into a bookshop). This used to be called "Monsieur de Paris," meaning the path for executioners. Go past the bookshop until you are in front of The Office of the Keeper, also known as "Concierge," who admits prisoners for imprisonment or torture and advises them on local restaurants—somehow! Look beyond and find your way through its entrance to another holding cell next door where condemned convicts could freshen up before their last public appearances, awaiting outside open cars named 'tumbrel,' which would drive them off on a final journey by guillotine to Place de la Concorde.

The Conciergerie is thus a ghostly, attractive place dedicated to torture, where those destined for death awaited their fate.

Above, a memorial chamber displays the names of 2,780 citizens condemned to death by the guillotine. Although several prominent names have been defaced (Charlotte Corday, Robespierre, or Louis XVI), you can still spot Marie Antoinette's name (on the opposite side of the entry on row 10 that reads Capet Marie-Antoinette). Go further down the corridor, and you will come across more gloomy cells, showing how overcrowded they were. Walk downstairs to the ground floor, where there is a small chapel hidden behind heavy gray curtains because it is built on the site of her cell.

The three paintings in this church tell us the sad story of Maria Antonia: her final greeting to her weeping family; waiting for her fate; and kneeling before receiving the Last Sacrament just a few hours before she was executed.

In "Court de femmes," women prisoners used to come out here for some fresh air. Look up and see the spikes above; these are remnants of bad times. Consider yourself fortunate, as an enemy of the state would leave here headless. On October 16th, 1793, Marie Antoinette got into a cart, which slowly transported her to Place de la Concorde to meet Monsieur de Paris.

When outside again, take your left through Boulevard du Palais. You'll find the city's oldest public clock, dating back to 1334, on this corner. Turn left at Quai de l'Horloge and walk along it beside the Seine River.

There is Pont Neuf right ahead of us, where our journey terminates. Take the first turn down into a peaceful triangular square called...

Place Dauphine

It is amazing how much charm there is right in the middle of Paris. With two million people, neighborhoods exist in Paris, each bearing the atmosphere of a village. The French Supreme Court building appears like an enormous marble gavel at the back. Enjoy a more neighborhood feel of Paris' village here at the park. Consult the "Eateries Along this Walk" section that was referred to earlier for recommendations on where to eat around here.

Carry on through Place Dauphine. When you reach its other end, you will be greeted by Henry IV (1553-1610). While not as famous as his grandson Louis XIV, Henry IV helped transform Paris into a European capital with such features as elegant architecture (e.g., the Louvre's Grand Gallery), serene squares (for example, Place Dauphine), and magnificent bridges (like Pont Neuf, which lies just to your right). You can step out onto the ancient bridge and take a momentary stop at a small alcove halfway across.

Pont Neuf and the Seine

Despite its name meaning "new bridge," this is actually among Paris' oldest structures, built during Henry IV's rule around 1600. Its arches span over the widest part of the river. Unlike other bridges, Pont Neuf was not made up of houses or any buildings whatsoever. The original intention for turrets was to host vendors and street performers only. Looking downstream from this bridge across to your left bank, you see that pedestrian-only Pont des Arts is coming next; farther ahead on your right bank lies the vast Louvre museum, while beyond it on your left bank stands Orsay Museum. Then what is that tall black tower from afar?

Our walk concludes where Paris began—along the Seine River—500 miles flowing from Dijon city till it reaches the English Channel and flows eastward along the heart of Paris itself. While shallow and slow within the city, the river's steep stone embankments (built-in 1910) needed to tame occasional floods.

In summer, these riverside quays become beaches, with locals sunbathing on lounge chairs, forming Paris Plages (see Sights chapter). Tourist boats and commercial barges hauling twenty percent of Paris' wares are visible all year. And along the shorelines, residents toss lines into waters where native Celts once fished.

We're done. You can try a boat trip from near the base of Pont Neuf island, however (Vedettes du Pont Neuf). The nearest metro stop is across the bridge on Right Bank at Pont Neuf. The number 69 bus travels east along Quai du Louvre (at the bridge's northern end) or west along Rue de Rivoli (one block northward). From here, you can go anywhere—this is central Paris.

LOUVRE MUSEUM

The journey through world history is offered by the famous museums of Paris, and the Louvre is an ideal starting point for your "art essay." The Louvre contains more than 30,000 pieces of art, cataloging Western civilization. Doing all this in one visit is impossible; hence, we shall concentrate on some highlights of the Louvre—Greek sculpture, Italian painting, and French painting.

Prehistoric stick figures until elegantly sculpted Venus de Milo and the dynamic Winged Victory of Samothrace visit Venus' representations across ages. There will also be a tour of calm medieval Madonnas, the mysterious Mona Lisa, and symbols of modern democracy. We would get important insights into their cultures and values by understanding what various civilizations considered beautiful.

Hours: Open Wednesday to Monday from 9:00 until 18:00; closed on Tuesdays. The last entry is 45 minutes before closing time. On Wednesdays and Fridays, the museum may extend hours. When to Go: Sundays, Mondays (the busiest), Wednesdays, and mornings are often crowded. When available, evening visits are usually less crowded.

Renovations: Anticipate corrections for renovation purposes as some sections may be closed one day per week or room numbers might change hereafter specified rooms during this tour.

Cost: €17 for a timed-entry ticket purchased online in advance (included with Museum Pass). Tickets allow entrance to special exhibitions but do not allow reentry after leaving the security check area between museum wings.

Reserved Entry Time Required: You must reserve a time slot even if you have a Museum Pass. Reservations can generally be made up until a few hours before your visit, but it is better to book at least one whole day ahead.

Buying Tickets/Passes at the Louvre: If you arrive without a ticket or reservation (not advisable), you might still be able to purchase a €15 timed-entry ticket during very quiet times (in a side room under the pyramid). The "Museum Pass Tabac" (La Civette du Carrousel) sells the Museum Pass at no extra charge (cash only). It is located in the underground Carrousel du Louvre mall; follow the Museum Pass signs inside the mall.

How to get there

The nearest Métro stop is the Palais Royal-Musée du Louvre. For buses, go along the Seine River eastbound with No. 69 and get off at Quai François Mitterrand. Westbound No.69 stops right in front of the iconic pyramid. There is also a taxi point on Rue de Rivoli near to the Palais Royal-Musée du Louvre. Métro station Bicycle rental stations are also available within its vicinity as an ecological option.

Entry: Probably, you will enter through what seems to be the most impressive entrance at each corner of this monumental complex—under the central courtyard's main pyramid. Bypassing ticket-type queues When you have your timed-entry ticket in hand, proceed straight inside. Alternatively, you can use a quieter entrance from an underground mall, which leads directly into the Carrousel du Louvre shopping complex. This entrance is accessible via 99 Rue de Rivoli, which connects directly with the Palais Royal-Musée du Louvre Métro stop (exit Musée du Louvre-Le Carrousel du Louvre) or through the Tuileries Garden gate close to Triumphal Arch. Inside the mall, head towards the inverted pyramid near the security checkpoint of the Louvre instead of following signs to the passengers' entrance since it involves going roundabouts.

Tours: Guided tours in English that typically leave at 11:00 (and sometimes at 14:00) are held below the pyramid in the Accueil des Groupes area and last for approximately one and a half hours during peak seasons. Booking these tours in advance, preferably online, is a good idea (€12 plus admission; call +33 1 40 20 52 63 for reservations). There are five-euro multimedia guides that can be hired to give detailed commentaries on some seven hundred great works of art.

Tour Duration: Allow yourself at least two hours.

Baggage Storage: Under the pyramid, there are self-service lockers where one can leave his bags. No big bags should go into the museum halls except small day bags.

Facilities: Restrooms are under the pyramid, but few are within the galleries themselves.

Dining Options: Several restaurants can be found at The Louvre, such as Café Mollien, which is located towards the end of the tour and has a view terrace where you can look down on the glass pyramid. On top of this, if you desire something less formal, there is a Richelieu wing that houses an escalator that leads to a self-service cafeteria. Moreover, Bistrot Benoit, situated beneath the pyramid, offers an alternatively more luxurious dining experience. Also, on its upper level, there's a food court within Carrousel du Louvre mall offering fast-food options.

For instance, after your visit, cafes like Café le Nemours (2 Place Colette), $$$ Le Fumoir (6 Rue de l'Amiral de Coligny), or Café la Palette (43 Rue de Seine across les Bouquinistes) would make excellent choices for dinner.

Highlights:

Ensure you do not miss Venus de Milo, Winged Victory, Mona Lisa, and other works by Leonardo da Vinci, Michelangelo, and Raphael, as well as French artists and many more of Western art's iconic figures.

It is a sprawling palace shaped like a U that is divided into three parts, of which the Louvre is the largest museum in the Western Hemisphere. On its north side is the Richelieu wing, which showcases Near Eastern artifacts, decorative arts, and French, German, and Northern European art. The Sully wing on its east side houses one of the largest collections of French paintings as well as ancient Egyptian and Greek art. We will focus mainly on the south-side wings (Denon and Sully), in which there are numerous works such as ancient Greek sculptures, Italian Renaissance paintings, and French Neo-Classical/Romantic art. Let it be known that the Louvre itself is immense, for it keeps changing all the time: rooms close down or change numbers; pieces may be out on loan or under restoration. Highlight priority while attempting to keep enough energy for exploration after finishing this tour of highlights only. Upon exiting from the pyramid, proceed to Denon's wing. Take the escalator up once. Present the ticket at the entrance, followed by 25 steps forward, then take the first left down, following signs towards Antiquités Grecques, till you reach Salle (Room) 170 with a brick ceiling: Grèce Préclassique above a sign heading Prehistory.

Greece, 3000 B.C.

Pre-classical Hellenic statues are solemn yet crude. The initial glass cases are Barbie dolls, which were made around 3 millennia before the pyramids rose in Egypt. These pre-rational figurines reduce women to their essential traits. Halfway down this hallway stands a diminutive female figure (Dame d'Auxerre) representing steadfastness, while another woman nearby named Core happens to be little more than an upright post with breasts. These statues are in a standing position: hands at sides, facing forward with rudimentary muscles and blank expressions. "Do not move." Early Hellenes, who admired such statues, preferred stability to motion. In 450 BC, Greece entered its Golden Age, an epoch of cultural creativity that would change the world. Over the next 500 years, Greek art became logical, structured, and harmonious. Beauty is in the balance between timeless stability and momentary movement. Most of the art from or inspired by Greece is found at the Louvre.

Let's go find one of the ancient world's most beautiful sculptures. Exit through the pre-Classical Greece galleries' far end, then climb up one more flight of stairs. At its top, turn left (towards eleven o'clock, pass through a domed room), then continue into the Sully Wing. After approximately fifty yards, turn right into Salle 345, where you will see Venus de Milo above a crowd of admirers below her. It has been suggested that this was the first statue to disarm onlookers among warlike Greeks.

Venus de Milo is also known as Aphrodite.

This love goddess caused a stir when she was discovered on Melos, an island in Greece, in 1820. Europe had already fallen for classical antiquity, and it seemed that this sculpture embodied all about ancient Greece itself. The Greeks depicted their gods as humans (which suggests humans are divine); hence, Venus' well-proportioned body reflects the Greek cosmos as being balanced and ordered.

Split Venus

Vertically, and see how both halves show the likeness. In the contrapposto pose, Venus stands on her right leg before raising her left leg to set her whole body in motion. When the left leg goes up, then the right shoulder dips. As one knee faces one direction, her head turns the other way for a balanced S-curve (also seen from behind).

Her smooth, textured top half is juxtaposed by the rough-hewn texture of her dress (size 14). She is two separate pieces of stone that have been joined at the hips (the seam is visible). The face looks like it could be real and anatomically correct but also idealized—i.e., so generic and faultless as to be a goddess. It isn't one woman; it's all women—the Greeks loved those perfectly formed features.

What are our missing arms doing? Some say that she raised her left arm while holding her dress with her right one. Others think that she was embracing some statue or leaning against a column. I go for "she was picking my belly button." Go around Venus. From every side, this is an intriguing statue that differs from others you see in the room. Later, we shall encounter it again from behind. Now come back to us again. Follow where Venus looks. Look around this long corridor.

Gallery of Statues

Greek sculptures pay homage to the human physique at its greatest. Artistic anatomy has been properly developed, and their poses are often relaxed and natural. In about the fifth century BC, Greek sculptors learned how to capture figures in motion rather than just frontal views. The classic contrapposto pose—in which weight falls upon one limb—achieves a synthesis between eternal stability and fleeting movement.

In this gallery, there are statues of gods, satyrs, soldiers, athletes, and common folk doing common things. Athenians' favorite deity was Athena. Protectors of Athens wore helmets and had (missing) spears, and Athena was no exception. She is shown ready to defend her city in a warrior's outfit. On one side of the hall, opposite the end, stands the colossal statue of Athena—the goddess of wisdom confronting that of love (Venus de Milo). Despite the subject matter, Golden Age artists strived for perfect harmony between human beings with their imperfections and weaknesses on the one hand and idealized Greek gods on the other.

Parthenon Friezes, mid-fifth century BC

Move on to Salle 347 (also known as Salle de Diane), located at the rear end of Venus de Milo. (Facing Venus, locate Salle 347 on your right, backtracking the way you came.) On each wall, there are two carved slabs. These pieces of stone were once part of Athens' Parthenon graveyards, which were built at their peak in Greece during its golden era. The position where these panels would have been hung is shown by the model of the Parthenon. A centaur panel could have been hung over the door, while a panel showing young women should be put under the roofed colonnade but above the door (to see it crouch down and look up in the model).

On the right side of this room, a Centaur harasses a woman as they desecrate ordinary people. But humans fought back and chased away their enemies. It depicted Athens overcoming the Persians.

The other relief shows the annual procession of sacred young girls who carried an embroidered shawl to Athena's 40-foot statue for four years in a row. All this is done on a few stone inches, and they look very real. They flow horizontally (the waistbands and the shoulders are horizontal), and their clothes cascade down vertically along the folds of the cloth. The guy at the center is relaxed, natural, and in a contrapposto pose. Look at the veins in his arm. Their pleated skirts make the girls stable like fluted columns, while their arms and legs come out naturally—human shapes emerge from stone with grace.

Roman Detour (Salles 409–418)

Go back twenty feet after turning toward Salle 409 or the Roman Antiquities section (Antiquités Romaines). Wander among Caesars; see if you can penetrate through their public personae. Apart from the myriad faces of Emperor Inconnu ("unknown"), there also appears to be Auguste as the first emperor, Augustus himself, and his scheming wife Livie, Livia. It was her son Tibère who was Caesar, "to whom Jesus Christ was rendered unto." Caligula was infamously perverse; Curly Domitia killed her husband; Hadrian made beards popular at the height of the Empire; and Marc Aurèle stoically presided over Rome's downward unrolling.

The Romans, who were pragmatic between 500 BC and AD 500, excelled in military strategies but produced less impressive works of art. This realistic approach was best seen in the creation of portrait busts of emperors venerated as gods on earth. For this reason, they copied several Greek statues to embellish their houses in Rome, temples, and other buildings.

190 BC Winged Victory, Samothrace

Keep going around the Roman collection until you get to the bottom of the stairs leading up to the first floor, where you will see a dramatic piece called Winged Victory Samothrace. She was situated on a hilltop island commemorating a naval victory, perched on the prow of a ship with windswept garments and sea-sprayed clothes clinging to her body. Her right arm originally extended high in celebration, like a Super Bowl winner, making the wave "We are number one.".

This is the Hellenistic Venus de Milo from c. 325 BC when Alexander the Great transmitted Athenian culture throughout the Mediterranean Sea Basin. The eagle is pushing against her wings, folded back by the wind, while she strides ahead with both feet securely planted but with wings (and arms) missing. Her clothes billow around her while she projects vertical strength. Consequently, these two opposing forces give this sculpture frozen energy.

This would have been considered an ugly statue by earlier Greeks during their golden age. It is rippling with life, unlike Parthenon maidens or Venus, which are delicately chiseled and blurred epitomes of beauty. You are left hanging by its unstable pose, just like an unfinished tune. In the meantime, Hellenistic Greeks cherished such performances that depicted real-life struggles for immortality among mortals.

A few years after finding out that it should be restored through an excavation process, they discover another part of it: Victory's open right hand sticking out one finger (1950). Due to its Turkish origin, the French entered into negotiations with the Turkish government to have it repatriated. After Turkey had lost many other ancient artifacts to France, it made sense that they would flip the bird at them.

Go into the octagonal room on the left and, facing Winged Victory, look up at Icarus, who seems to be bungee jumping from above. Look out of a window towards the pyramid.

The Louvre as a Palace

The Louvre was originally a palace, having been built in stages over seven centuries. In current terms, you are looking at what used to be the Sully wing (the side over your right shoulder when facing the pyramid), which was once a medieval fortress. Then came Tuileries Palace, about 500 yards away, beyond the victory arch and the pyramid's open space today. Successive kings kept expanding the north and south wings of both buildings until they finally met. Three centuries later, the two palaces were connected, giving rise to the elongated rectangular Louvre in 1852; meanwhile, fire gutted the U-shaped Tuileries Palace during a riot after only nineteen years.

The glass pyramid in front of you is called I.M. Pei's creation (1989). However, Parisians initially hated this prism as much as another controversial innovation one hundred years before: The Eiffel Tower.

The plaque at the base of the dome in the Octagon room has it. The inscribed words are as follows: "Le Musée du Louvre, fondé le 16 September 1792." France's Revolutionary National Assembly, which killed their king, also established this museum. What more logically could have been done? Kill the king, take over his residence and his art as yours, and then let people in; this is this is Europe's first public museum.

The Apollo Gallery

It is a glimpse into the inner world of Versailles-like luxury French kings' residences before Louis XIV came up with his palace. Imagine a candlelit soirée in this space decorated with stucco and gold leaf, featuring tapestries portraying important Frenchmen alongside pictures showing mythological and symbolic events. Crystal vases, marquetry tables, and other numerous art objects testify to the wealth of France, which was for two centuries Europe's leading power. There are portraits on the wall representing notable French rulers such as Henri IV, who built Pont Neuf; Louis XIV, who was known as the Sun King; and François I, who brought Leonardo da Vinci (and the Italian Renaissance) to France.

Walk past cases filled with royal tableware at one end of the room. The glass case shows off some of the crown jewels. The collection changes, but you may see jewel-laden crowns like those of Louis XV or the less gaudy Crown of Charlemagne plus a 140-carat Regent Diamond that adorned crowns worn by Louis XVI, Louis XV, and Napoleon once upon a time.

The Medieval World (1200–1500)

A rare toilet (WC) stands not far away next to Salle 650 near Sully Wing. The Italian collection (Peintures Italiennes) is on the other side of Winged Victory. Go back towards Winged Victory, cross over again, and enter Denon Wing/Room 706, where two frescoes by Botticelli will show you how ancient Greece was "reborn" in the Renaissance. Proceed into Salle 708.

Almost every European church had a painting like this during the Age of Faith (1200s). More than anyone else, Mary was a cult figure—more popular even than Madonna in the late 20th century—which made her adored by many people who prayed to her as she bore Baby Jesus. After the fall of the Roman Empire around AD 500, medieval Europe became a barren and dangerous place where the only constant presence was the Christian Church.

Altarpieces usually followed this pattern: solemn iconic faces, rigid poses, elegant drapery folds, and generic angels. Cimabue's holy figures are laid out flat against a gold field as if they were made from cut paper while existing in a golden ethereal realm that could not be imagined as real human beings living on our darkly sinful earth.

Giotto, St. Francis of Assisi, Receiving the Stigmata, c. 1295–1300

On an Italian hillside strewn with rocks kneels Francis of Assisi (c. 1181–1226), an itinerant monk feeling sympathy for Jesus' agony and death. Suddenly he looked up to see Christ Himself above him; he had six wings spread out wide to cover his body. He shone beams from his wounds towards his empathetic monk on hands, feet, and into the side, branding him with stigmata wounds too. Francis went ahead to bring the Renaissance spirit into Middle Ages Europe. Artists such as Giotto were inspired by his humble love for mankind and nature, which made them depict actual human beings feeling genuine emotions within their surroundings full of beauty while alive.

He doesn't just tell us what happened as a good filmmaker; Giotto (c. 1266–1337) is like a master director who makes us see the event in the present tense, stopping the scene at its most exciting instant. His style, which has nothing to do with realism, causes his paintings to be perceived as though they were filmed in slow motion. The work's perspective is sketchy—Francis' dwelling place is smaller than his, and Christ concentrates on Francis but faces us somehow—but Giotto's ability to make an image feel real goes beyond this simplicity, producing a foreground (Francis), middle distance (his hut), and background (hillside). On a predella or the bottommost part of an altarpiece panel where this picture was taken, some birds have gathered near Saint Francis' feet for an expected word about God.

Italian Renaissance (1400-1600)

Some of the greatest and some not-so-great works of Italian Renaissance painting are on display in the long Grand Gallery. This was built in the late 1500s to connect the old palace with the Tuileries Palace, and it has a lot of Italy's Renaissance art pieces that this museum is famous for. The challenge is to look towards the far end from where you are standing at the entrance. I hold a world record for having walked through the entire length of the gallery with a high-heel toe action on my feet as a tourist and completed it within 1:58 minutes (only two were injured). You can try it out yourself to see how long it will take you. In passing, I recognized some of these attributes appearing in Italian Renaissance paintings.

- **Symmetrical**: Madonna paintings have saints' figures arranged beside them—saints on either side, such as two or more.

- **Realistic**: Some features, like human faces, look pretty much like we see them every day.

- **Three-Dimensional**: Each scene contains huge areas showing distance horizons.

- **Religious**: Many Madonnas, children, martyrs, and saints.

- **Classical**: There happen to be certain Greek gods and classical nudes here, but even Christian saints have been sculpted in Greek poses, while Mary assumes a Venus-like posture that embodies all Christian virtues presented through her face and gestures.

Leonardo da Vinci, The Virgin and Child with St. Anne, 1510

This pyramid, with the grandmother at its base, and the mother in the middle position while the baby occupies one corner, characterizes the three generations represented by these women. Leonardo puts their bodies into action, which is contained within this perfectly balanced structure. One foot points leftward (is this Mona Lisa?) and her daughter Mary reaches rightward from her sitting position on her mother's knee. Jesus looks teasingly at Mother while his head twists away. And finally, Lamb falls away backward from him, sadly.

Nevertheless, the scene remains peaceful amid all this commotion. As ordered is the world of Renaissance god, so is this geometrically perfect universe.

Raphael, La Belle Jardinière, c. 1507

This artist has taken his lead from Leonardo by developing an idealized style of painting. The Madonna, Child, and John the Baptist arrangement also happens to be a balanced pyramid with some kind of ethereal charm. Christ's mother, meanwhile, has a look that speaks of maternal love (the title means 'The Beautiful Gardener') and looks at her son tenderly as she holds his hand in a gesture symbolizing oneness between them. Jesus stares upwards, innocently taking up contrapposto like one of those chubby Greek statues. Baby John the Baptist kneels lovingly on Jesus' feet with a cross clutched firmly to his chest, which indirectly suggests that he will die on behalf of this playmate in the future too. Intertwining gestures and gazes give intimacy to this masterpiece and make it look complete while blended with Raphael's iridescently smooth brushstrokes.

It was with Raphael that the Greek standard for beauty attained its climax during the revival period known as the Renaissance; henceforth, imitation persisted—sugar-coated Madonnas whose merit can sometimes overshadow his genius—but let us not lessen what is undeniably his defining work here.

Da Vinci, Leonardo, Mona Lisa, 1503–1506.

A short walk from the venue will get you to Salle 711, where you will find the Mona Lisa (La Joconde). On her artificial wall and behind the glass, she stands apart in isolation. She is easily noticeable by anyone following signs or a crowd; it's the only painting you can hear. (It may smell like humanity if too many people come here.) When Francis I invited da Vinci to France, he traveled with light baggage, having carried just a few of his paintings along. One of them was that of Lisa del Giocondo, who was a wealthy Florentine merchant's wife. François immediately fell in love with this picture and made it the anchor point for the small Italian collection that has evolved into the Louvre Museum in three centuries. He named it La Gioconda (La Joconde), a play on both her last name and an Italian word for "happiness." But we call it Mona Lisa—an abbreviation of Italian words meaning "my missis Lisa."

Mona may not meet your expectations; she is less big than thought, darker, sunken in the huge room, and hidden under a shiny pane of windows. So why all the commotion? Let's have a closer look at this famous artwork... For instance, any lover should accept his or her object of adoration for what he or she is rather than what they expect him or her to be.

Firstly, however, one cannot escape noticing that smile that made Leonardo known throughout the world. Leonardo created an unclear effect called sfumato that blurred out outline edges near her enigmatic smile. You cannot even determine exactly how her lips stretch outwards or curl upwards towards either cheekbone. Is it glee? Misery? Love? Or just some stupid model's smile?? Everyone understands these feelings differently, thereby transferring their emotions about her secretive visage. These are Rorschach blots…so, how old are you?

The following should be looked past by someone keen to get a sense of the smile, the eyes that seem to follow one (like many painted eyes do), and other subtle elements of the Renaissance that make this painting work. The body shocks as it appears much more than flesh and blood but rather like a statue, which is also in perfect equilibrium and a pyramid with mass displayed obliquely. Her arm is gently laid down on the armrest of her chair, just at the edge of the frame, as if she is sitting there looking through the window at us. Her sleeves droop downward; her hands dangle loosely together—such crude representations of clothes' folds never came true. The characteristic of Leonardo's landscape depicts distance by becoming more and more unclear.

This portrait has been generally recognized as Lisa del Giocondo, but some other theories regarding its subject have appeared, including that it may be Leonardo himself or even Mama Lisa. For example, during an infrared scan done not so long ago, there were some scarce traces of the veil over Mona's dress, which could have meant (as it was usual for those times) childbirth.

It feels serene and balanced overall while still maintaining some secrecy around it. Mona is subtly smiling with a distant beauty that draws people in without being entirely accessible, like just snatches of street music from a metro corridor. This is something different from overpowering, but she will give you a wink, provided you know what patience means.

Paolo Veronese, The Marriage at Cana, 1562–1563.

Before leaving Mona behind, you look back at the paparazzi-type scenario happening all around you right now. On the opposite side of the Mona Lisa, there's Take ten steps back from this big canvas, where your whole sightline comprises only this picture. And suddenly…you're invited to join! Go get yourself a glass of wine. It is this ideal of Renaissance-loving beauty at any cost.

Within the context of a spacious setting characterized by Renaissance architecture, multi-colored gentlemen and women adorned in their best attire eat and drink while musicians animate the merrymaking. The food is made ready for eating by attendants, jesters entertain, and animals roam around. In the upper left, a dog and its owner watch. A strong man wearing yellow pours out wine from a jug (right foreground). The man in white tastes some, thinking, "Hmm, that's not bad," while nearby an enraged feline combats with a lion. Almost forgotten is the bridal couple on the extreme left side.

It may be hard to believe, but this is a religious work portraying Jesus' wedding feast, where he converted water into wine. In the very center of the 130 celebrants stands Jesus, who perhaps wonders whether a soft drink would have been better instead. Like all other Italian people who lived during the Renaissance period, the Venetians thought that Christ was part of them, i.e., that those who loved created things as much as he did.

Through Mona's exit to Salle Denon (Room 701). On your left, there is a romantic room with drama, and on your right, you will see the grand Neoclassical room. Kneel before the Louvre's largest canvas after passing through Salle Daru, Room 702, which is a Neoclassical room entered before this one.

French Painting (1780–1850)

Napoleon, whose parents were common people, snatches the crown of an empire and prepares to declare himself the emperor of a "New Rome." Having been crowned empress by him first, Napoleon sends off the pope from Rome to officiate. As he thought nobody deserved that, Napoleon himself took over and allowed the pope to depart frustrated.

After the French people executed their king in 1793 during the Revolution, Democracy struggled in its infancy amid chaos. It was Napoleon Bonaparte—a charismatic and brilliant young general—who stepped forward to unify France. He insisted on being crowned an Emperor on his conquests of most parts of Europe rather than just a King. The historic coronation was immortalized by painter Jacques-Louis David (pronounced dah-VEED).

In the picture's background, there is a radiant woman who stands out, though she is not there for real. Though Napoleon's mother had missed it all, David had been ordered to paint her into it anyway—depicting this within the artwork frame. The ceremony occurred at Notre Dame Cathedral, where faux columns and arches made visitors feel like they were in Greece or Rome.

David served as either Napoleon's official artist or propagandist, organizing colors and designs for public events. (Try finding David's self-portrait with curly gray hair on a second balcony, peeping around the tassel above Napoleon's crown.) The neoclassical style that influenced future artists emerged from David's clear, simple manner using Greek themes.

La Grande Odalisque (1814) by Jean-Auguste-Dominique Ingres, along your way back towards the Romantic room, is another horizontal version of Venus de Milo's behind. Keep going through Salle Denon into Room 700, full of French Romanticism.

Théodore Géricault, The Raft of the Medusa, 1819

Neoclassicism presented itself as a thinking art movement that opposed emotional Romanticism. It was at its peak in the early 19th century, when it emphasized motion and emotion.

One vivid illustration of this is a scene of a dramatic shipwreck. Their twisted shapes illustrate the turmoil as bodies and desperate souls cling to their raft. The ripples on muscles, seething clouds, and stormy seas are evident. On the right-hand side, there is a green corpse hanging overboard. To the left side, a man holds a dead body; his face shows total despair after weeks adrift.

The story was based on an actual event: when they were shipwrecked, 150 people suffered twelve days of privation, which resulted in cannibalism with only fifteen survivors. Motivated to shock public opinion, young artist Géricault (pronounced ZHAIR-ee-ko) interviewed survivors and studied them in morgues and asylums so that he could express their misery.

Yet out of such despair comes hope. There is a pyramid of bodies reaching up to one that waves a flag at the topmost point. They desperately signal to a distant ship—their last hope—that eventually rescues them. It speaks volumes about how art can move people's hearts.

Eugène Delacroix, Liberty Leading the People, 1831

In 1830, Charles X issued an oppressive edict for which he received condemnation from his subjects. Parisians went all Les Miz-like in responding against royal oppression during this revolt by succeeding in replacing him with Louis-Philippe, who ruled under a modern constitution. A hard proletarian with a sword among rebels, an intellectual in a top hat carrying a shotgun, and the little boy with guns represent some rebel group amongst them.

The heroine herself waving the French flag leads them through such confusion; it resembles Winged Victory but without wings or wearing anything on her upper body since she is half naked.

Delacroix (pronounced del-ah-kwah) uses a triad of colors—red, white, and blue—that represent France to create strong emotions. It is this painting that emboldens France as the symbol of modern democracy. This symbolizes freedom and is therefore a befitting tribute to the Louvre, the first-ever museum for the public. The good things in life, including art, belong to everybody, not just a few rich ones. Thus, this masterpiece echoes the country's motto: Liberté, Égalité, Fraternité.

Go beyond Café Mollien at the far end of this room and then walk downstairs. Here you will find an impressive reclining male statue that seems to have woken up from centuries- of sleep.

Michelangelo, Slaves, 1513-1515

And so these sculptures by one of the world's greatest sculptors effectively bring together ancient and contemporary eras in a museum journey. Michelangelo, like his Italian Renaissance contemporaries, had been influenced by Greek art. These works could easily have emerged two thousand years ago with their perfect anatomy, dynamic poses, and idealized features.

The Dying Slave (sometimes referred to as the Sleeping Slave, who appears to be almost lying on a bed) turns languidly against his simple restraints, exposing his smooth, unmarked skin. Notice how neatness defines that rippling, well-toned left arm in contrast with the rough details of the face and neck. Within Michelangelo's work lies a tale about the body itself. It is probably Michelangelo's most erotic nude sculpture—a master study of maleness.

A rebellious slave struggles against his bonds. His head twists one way while his leg turns another way around [ungrammatical: turn what?].

He gazes upward, trying to free himself even from the marble stone itself that he was made from. As God had placed them inside him, Michelangelo regarded it as his duty to remove marble from the bodies of these enslaved ones. This slave embodies the agony of that process and the ecstasy of the result.

End of tour

These statues may be trapped within this building, but you are free to leave. Your visit to the Louvre has reached its climax as you immerse yourself in great artworks through the ages. Reflect for a moment on how far you have come, from ancient sculptures to revolutionary paintings. For exit, turn right and follow signs downstairs to Sortie, where Paris awaits with more delights.

EIFFEL TOWER

This is a crowded and expensive place, with other viewpoints in Paris that are arguably better, yet it remains an experience of great value to see these one thousand-foot-tall structures. The Mona Lisa can seem disappointing to some people, but not the Eiffel Tower, which rarely fails to impress, even if there are many skyscrapers now. You only have one chance in your life to do this. The thrilling climb up and down provides you with a sensation that makes you feel like an integral part of the community of over 250 million visitors who have made the Eiffel Tower one of the most visited monuments in recent times. Furthermore, besides having incredible views, the tower is symbolic of all that characterizes Paris.

Price: €27 will take you to the third level; €17.50 for elevator access to either the first or second level; €11 to climb stairs for the first or second levels; and €21 includes stair climbing plus elevator usage up to the summit. Entrance into the summit lift must be paid for before entering the lift area. These fees are not among those covered by the Museum Pass.

Timings: It opens from 9:00–24:45 daily between mid-June and August and from 9:30–23:45 from September to mid-June. The last elevator ride up stops at 22:30; lower levels open till midnight throughout the year except for the last admission at 23:00 on stairs during September–mid-June when the last entrance is at approximately 18:30 approx. Also, note that it may close temporarily due to high winds at its top, but ticket holders are still allowed in unless weather conditions are unsafe.

Details can be found at www.toureiffel.paris/en.

Ticket Tips

Advance Tickets Recommended: A reservation is vital, especially if you want an elevator ride since this eliminates waiting time as well as queuing costs when buying tickets directly through the internet, where one can choose the entry time and skip the waiting line. Tickets that include stairs are only available on-site. Tickets can be purchased online up to 60 days in advance, starting at 8:30 a.m. Paris time; however, they usually sell out quite rapidly from April to September. In case no spaces are left, a "lift entrance ticket with access to the 2nd floor" is also good because the view from there is great as well. Another way of getting a ticket may be to check the website again about a week before your visit. The ticket for those who want to go all the way up has "Lift entrance ticket with access to the summit" written on it.

Buying tickets On-Site: Sometimes you can just come and enter immediately, but often there are long queues, especially on weekends and holidays. Without any reservation, it is better to arrive at least 30 minutes before the opening hours, as it takes that much time for security check-in procedures, which start half an hour before the tower opens, and then queue for tickets themselves. Alternatively, you can visit later in the day when there is less traffic or crowds, such as after 7 p.m. from May through August or after 5–6 p.m. out of tourist season (in winter, it gets dark by around 17).

When to Visit

Optimal Timing: Come early enough so that you have some daylight left to see panoramic views and stay until dusk for the stunning lights below.

How to Get There

Transport: The Eiffel Tower is a short ten-minute walk from either the Bir-Hakeim or Trocadéro Métro stops, or Champ de Mars-Tour Eiffel RER/Train-C station. The Ecole Militaire Métro stop by Rue

Cler is twenty minutes away on foot. For bus options, buses #42, #69, and #86 are available within reach.

Process of Entry

Safety: Security at the tower involves walls made of glass around it. Accessing the tower is free, though it requires going through security, which resembles airport screening and may take more than 30 minutes during busy periods.

With Reservations: Arrive at the entrance at least 30 minutes before your scheduled entry time. After the security check, there should be green signs labeled "Visiteurs avec Réservation" (Visitors with Reservation).

Without Reservations: Once at the gate after security check, go to ticket booths with yellow banners and follow signs pointing out "Individuels" or "Visiteurs sans Tickets."

For Stair Access: You can buy tickets directly on the south pillar marked for stair entry.

Tour Duration

Time Required: With a booking and a light crowd, you can do up and down (almost no sightseeing) in about 90 minutes. Otherwise, leave three to four hours if you have to wait in line, make your way to the top as well, and come take a look down below.

Safety Measures

Baggage Limitations: Oversized bags measuring more than 19 inches long by 8 inches wide by 12 inches deep are not allowed into the premises, and there's no place to keep them.

Facilities Provided

Washrooms: Free toilets are located at ground level behind the east pillar of the Tower. Inside Tower consolation for all levels has large queues most times.

Places to Eat at

Restaurants in the Eiffel Tower: There are also two four-diamond **$$$$** restaurants on the tower with beautiful views. Reservations at either restaurant will enable you to skip the initial elevator line (make them well in advance). However, you still have to go through a security checkpoint and cannot enter more than 15–30 minutes before your reservation time (though you may stay beyond that).

The first floor's 58 Tour Eiffel (+33 1 72 76 18 46), while the more expensive Le Jules Verne is located on the second level (+33 1 45 55 61 44).

Picnic Option: Consider picking up picnic supplies from shops near the Ecole Militaire Métro stop and dining in the Champ de Mars park.

Choose side grassy areas or benches along the central lawn to eat your meal (the central area might be out of bounds).

Highlights

Spectacular Views: Enjoy breathtaking views of Paris and beyond.

View Points: There are three viewing platforms on the Eiffel Tower at about 200, 400, and 900 feet. The summit is windy but provides an unforgettable experience, while the second level offers the best view of Paris' landmarks. Other facilities at each level include displays, toilets, and other services, as well as souvenir shops.

Climbing Upstairs: For those who enjoy adventures, a staircase goes from the ground up to the first level (360 steps) and then to the second level (another 360 steps). Although enclosed in wire cages for safety reasons, a person suffering from vertigo can still get dizzy using them.

Complete Eiffel Tower Experience

To fully experience the Eiffel Tower, you have to begin at its bottom and work upwards. There is no single elevator that takes you directly to "le Sommet." First, ride an elevator or climb stairs to get to the second level. Some elevators stop at the first level, but it is easier to move back. The queue for another lift from this point up to the summit on the third floor. Descend back down after enjoying the view from above to explore more around the second floor, then walk down long stairs that take you back through sights located on the first floor. Finally, for exit purposes, use this last way out by going via descending flights of stairs leading down again from the top towards the ground.

Outside

From afar, the Eiffel Tower looks fragile and graceful, but it becomes huge upon scrutiny, even though somehow intimidating. The tower, along with its antenna, reaches a height of 1,063 feet, just slightly taller than New York's Chrysler Building, and has seventy-seven stories running into it. It covers an area measuring 3.5 acres, inclusive of its four support pillars, making a total weight of 7,300 tons of steel plus sixty tons of paint covering it in addition; however, they are so well engineered that their presence does not result in more pounds per square inch of pressure at the base than a linebacker trying to tiptoe.

Although it was once the tallest manmade structure ever built, there have been many other towers (including the Tokyo Skytree, which stands at 2,080 feet), radio masts (e.g., the KVLY-TV mast in North Dakota, which reaches 2,063 feet.), and skyscrapers (such as the Burj Khalifa in Dubai, United Arab Emirates, with its height of 2,717 feet).

Environs

The long green space south of this tower is known as Champ de Mars; originally a military practice ground for troops and students from the nearby military academy (Ecole Militaire), it is now serving as a public park too. To its north across the Seine lies Trocadéro, with a curved palace colonnade around a square.

Lifts and Steps

To cope with large numbers of visitors, the Eiffel Tower was designed with elevators when it was constructed. The only way up the slanting pillars of the tower, which were not vertical like those on most buildings glimpsed today, was by designing an elevator system that had never been seen before in history. Modern-day lifts make about one hundred round trips daily.

There are 1,665 steps leading to its top floor, although only 720 can be climbed to the second level by tourists. Incredibly, though, during the 1905 race, one person scaled from the bottom to the second level, almost a four-hundred-foot climb, within three minutes and twelve seconds.

The significance of the history

The first person to reach the 1889 Paris World's Fair walked beneath the "arch" of the Eiffel Tower, which had just been constructed, and into the fairgrounds, marking the centenary of the French Revolution and acknowledging France as an international state. Gustave Eiffel (1832–1923), a bridge constructor, won the contest to create a centerpiece for the fair, thereby outshining his rivals' proposals, including that of a gigantic guillotine.

Eiffel, who had worked hard on funding for this project, even deservedly made sure that it was named after him. He was involved in its design; he financed it himself, produced iron beams at his factory, and invented the special cranes and machinery needed to build it up. He managed to finish one before the deadline and within the budget set by the World's Fair organizing committee. Originally planned to be a temporary structure only, the Eiffel Tower, from a practical point of view, only showed that France could afford to build something better than any other country on earth at that time. Although it was intended for disassembly right after the exhibition was over, Parisians lobbied for its preservation.

To a generation fascinated by technology, this was an incredible marvel displaying progress and human intelligence. However, some people did not like it at all. Guy de Maupassant (1850–1893), a famous writer, chose to eat lunch inside the tower rather than see its face.

Over time, however, there have been different uses of the Eiffel Tower, such as radio transmission since 1909 till now; cosmic-ray observation in 1910; advertising board spelling "Citroën" from 1925–34; Nazi television programs during the 1940s under occupation until liberation by Americans in August 1944; launch pad numerous fireworks events; besides being used as a framework supporting spectacular light shows, the current arrangement dates back to the year 2000, when the Millennium Festival took place.

Climbing to the top

Take either of the stairs or an elevator to the second level, and then line up for another lift to reach the summit. Up at a height of 900 feet, it is very windy and offers panoramic views. On a clear day, you can see as far as 40 miles stretching out in a 360-degree view of Paris.

Third Level (Le Sommet)

Use maps with panoramic pictures from the top to identify Parisian landmarks. Looking westwards, locate a miniature Statue of Liberty at the other end of Seine's needle-like island, which gazes towards her larger replica in New York City over a distance of 3633 miles. Gustave Eiffel also created an internal framework for the Statue of Liberty in New York made from copper by Frederic Bartholdi, a fellow Frenchman, in 1886.

Construction

Visualize the builders constructing the Eiffel Tower; they are up there somewhere while assembling it. It required Industrial Age ingenuity: mass production, advanced technology, and substantial financial means.

The structure was built like an Erector set with 18,000 pieces, consisting of 15-foot iron beams and two-and-a-half million rivets. In two years, the tower was constructed by 300 workers who began building wooden support structures for the lower parts. Pillars converged as they rose so that, ultimately, the tower could stand on its own. Iron beams were hoisted by steam-powered cranes that even rolled along tracks on top of these pillars as they ascended. Workmen walked along them or dangled from rope ladders to drive in red-hot bolts, which cooled into solid rivets.

In just eighteen months of construction, it already exceeded the height of the Washington Monument (555 feet) and took thirty-six years to build. The tower was initially painted rusty red but has since changed colors over time, including mustard and now brown-gray. Every seven years, twenty-five full-time painters apply sixty tons of paint by hand spraying.

Two years, two months, and five days after beginning work on it, the Eiffel Tower was completed. On May 15th, 1889, a beacon lit atop it in red, white, and blue; the World's Fair opened; and the first amazed visitor traveled to its summit.

North View (Nord)

Looking northward will allow your eyes to experience the curved colonnade of Trocadero at your feet, where the World Fair happened in 1878. Across this lies Bois de Boulogne, a forested and vast park measuring three square miles, which is common ground for joggers during daylight hours and prostitutes at night. Alongside is the La Defense district, whose tall skyscrapers dominate the Paris horizon, while the iconic Arc de Triomphe is just to the right of the Trocadero area.

East View (Est)

Turning your gaze eastwards, you will be treated to a view of the many bridges crossing over the river Seine, including Pont Alexandre III, which has four gold statues on it. Thereafter, the Orsay Museum, Louvre, Pont Neuf, and twin towers of Notre Dame can be seen if you look upstream. On your left bank, Butte Montmartre's top is crowned by an elongated bullet shape.

South View (Sud)

Running from southward are several famous landmarks: the Champ de Mars, the Ecole Militaire, the Y-shaped UNESCO building, and the Montparnasse Tower at 689 feet. While in sunlight, the golden dome of Les Invalides stands on the left side.

The Summit

Climb up a couple of steps, and you're at the outer top beneath satellite dishes. Gustave Eiffel once had a small apartment. The original Edison phonograph was presented by Thomas Edison to Eiffel and his daughter Claire during the fair; this moment has been recreated with mannequins. (Then they cranked it up and blasted The Who's "I Can See for Miles.")

Second Level

At four hundred feet, this level delivers the best perspectives, allowing viewers to easily recognize city landmarks while remaining at a distance. The second floor consists of souvenir shops, toilets, and a little café. A world-famous Le Jules Verne restaurant owned by Frédéric Anton, highly rated French, offers high-class food that suits the place.

Take an elevator or walk down three hundred...

First Level

For instance, the height of 200 feet represents the first level that gives a good view as witnessed from the tower's viewing screens. A small concert hall, restaurant, and public area with a café, shop, and little theater are among the attractions found here. The charm is enhanced by seasonal pop-up restaurants and stalls, as well as child-friendly playgrounds. It is common to have an ice-skating rink at this level during the winter.

The glass floor is a thrilling one; it makes for a great place to take selfies. While standing on it, you feel like you might fall eighteen stories below you. All of these things are connected in some way—do you know what? Different temporary exhibitions inform visitors regarding how heating from solar radiation causes the topmost end of the tower to extend away from the sun by approximately five inches, hence why it sometimes seems to sway slightly when there are gusts of strong wind with its intricate framework design. Tolerating wind forces was Gustave Eiffel's objective in designing the structure so that it would only sway slightly instead of collapsing.

To go down, use either stairs or elevators (5 minutes, 360 steps). Usually, stairs are faster.

Back on the Ground

Finally, stroll over to Place du Trocadéro across the Seine or along Champ de Mars until the very last point. During the daytime, this building looks impressive, but at twilight, it turns into something fantastic, even if silent, while night falls upon Paris, which sits back and invites evening time for itself; every hour starts with a five-minute light show that leaves no one indifferent.

RUE CLER

Walking slowly along this busy market street is to be immersed in the essence of a live, old-fashioned neighborhood with its cultural distinctiveness. No matter how rich and dynamic it may become, Rue Cler has that ordinary ambiance that echoes throughout most of the other parts of Paris.

Shopping for food is the backbone of French daily life. Rue Cler has been pedestrianized since 1984 and is a string of essential shops selling wine, cheese, chocolate, and breads. When it comes to learning the art de vivre à la française, there's no better place than Rue Cler. You'll find numerous boutiques where you can pick out items for your perfect French picnic.

A Walk Down Rue Cler

Begin at the northern end of Rue Cler's walking mall, where it intersects with Rue de Grenelle (near bus stop #69 and an easy walk from Ecole Militaire metro station). Come during bustling market hours at Rue Cler (Tuesday-Saturday: 8:30 AM-1:00 PM and 3:00 PM-7:30 PM; Sunday morning until noon; closed Sunday afternoon and Monday). Set aside about an hour to leisurely explore this three-block stretch and enjoy some great café fare. For shopping etiquette tips in Paris, refer to the Shopping section in the Activities chapter.

1. Café Roussillon

Step outside this classic bar/café and soak up the atmosphere that characterizes any vibrant neighborhood around here. Ground floors are given over to retail, while upper stories serve as homes, giving rise to a lively atmosphere found hardly anywhere else in America's towns. Let's feel part of our community as we see people walking their dogs, pushing baby strollers, or carrying bags filled with everything imaginable. It is worth noting that Paris lives on its neighborhood culture, making Rue de Cler a good illustration of such charms due to its free-traffic shopping street.

Part local coffee shop, part drinking hole, the bar in Café Roussillon serves drinks at a cheaper rate for patrons standing at the counter. Have a look at the blackboard to see what wines are being served by the glass.

Just across the street, if you're looking for designer baby clothes, they're here at...

2. Petit Bateau

In France, parents frequently spend as much on their babies as their pets; therefore, they dress them in fashion clothing made by renowned designers. To cater to this trend of fashionable children's clothing, including their signature sailor-striped underwear, the chain store Petit Bateau exists.

France has gone from having one of Europe's oldest and smallest populations to boasting one of its highest birthrates, with two children born per couple on average, compared to 1.6 as the European average. The babies have become fashionable, and governments did offer substantial tax breaks to families who had children, thus making markets like Rue Cler appealing because they could still afford local farm produce.

3. Au Bon Jardinier (Titoled The Good Gardener)

Cross Rue de Grenelle and you will find Au Bon Jardinier, which is a great place for fresh fruits and veggies. Every morning, goods arrive here from Rungis Market near Paris' Orly Airport—Europe's largest— within an amazingly short period, judging by how many miles there are between these locations. Remember your grocery bag or two-wheeled cart since Parisians prefer not to use extra packaging materials out of environmental concerns.

Parisians are attuned to what is in season, and when it comes time for shopping, they often let their noses guide them through fruit and vegetable displays. Compare gariguettes—torpedo-shaped French strawberries—with foreign ones' smell; only then will you know the difference between the two varieties. Local people call Belgian strawberries "plastic" because they are red outside but white inside. Take a look at the herbs in that box towards the back row to see if today's delivery has come.

Close by lies a Franprix, a branch of a national chain supermarket, and across the street from the Grand Hôtel Lévêque is Traiteur Asiatique. As common as bakeries, these quick Asian food-to-go shops have greatly influenced traditional Parisian eating habits.

4. Café Evolution

Once it was a tobacco shop, this cozy café is where you can have a drink or take something light to eat while enjoying the view. This is an example that represents the changing face of the former working-class market street into an increasingly upmarket area. However, some residents mourned when traditional shops were replaced by trendy cafes.

5. Wine Bacchus

Just past the Grand Hôtel Lévêque, where you can find lots of wine varieties to go with your meal, is Wine Bacchus. Wines are organized by region, satisfying many Parisians who prefer wines from their birthplaces. In the store's center, you will get quality bottles, especially those on monthly specials for around €12. The knowledgeable staff helps in suggesting wines that match your menu and budget; they will also cool a bottle of white wine in "Le Chiller" within three minutes.

6. Fromagerie

Next door, you get the smell of cheese, which spills out onto the street from this cheese shop. The shop offers over 200 types of French cheese, including cow (vache) and goat (chèvre). Known as a crémerie or "BOF," it sells butter (beurre), eggs (oeuf), and cheese (fromage).

Observe how cheeses come in different shapes—triangles, cylinders, rounds, little hockey pucks—all covered with mold of various colors. Oftentimes, the shape indicates area origin, with pyramids usually hailing from the Loire Valley. It is this concept known as terroir—the unique combination of sun, soil, and generations of farming expertise—that imparts each cheese with its individuality. I once had a Parisian friend who said that the smell of one particularly pungent cheese was "the feet of angels."

The back room is filled with les meules—large wheels of cheese made from 250 gallons of milk, each weighing about 170 pounds. Even though the rind on small cheeses such as Camembert or Brie is edible, this is not the case with these giant ones. When you are dining out, consider having a cheese course either right before dessert or in place of dessert. A good cheese plate has hard cheese (such as Comté), soft cheese (like Brie or Camembert), blue cheese, and goat's milk cheese, ideally from different regions, with the strongest being last.

7. Poissonnerie

Across the street is the fishmonger's shop. Fresh fish arrives daily from ports on the English Channel into Paris and is sometimes fresher than in many coastal towns. Like other poissoneries in Paris, this place has had to upgrade to meet strict European hygiene regulations.

8. Former Boucherie Chevaline

Next door, there is an adorable Rue Cler storefront underneath an awning. The entrance's mosaic and glass advertise horsemeat: Boucherie Chevaline. Although no longer selling horse meat, this elegant 1930s storefront that bears the artist's name continues to be a piece of preserved history worthy of a museum but solidly rooted here.

9. À la Mère de Famille (desserts)

Just a few steps across the street from it is the A la Mère de Famille Confectionery. The shop, which has been in the neighborhood for 30 years, sells contemporary and traditional confections as well. "The old women want the same sweets that have made them happy for 80 years," says the owner. You can buy chocolates one by one for about €1 and build your box of assorted ones. Although chocolate was once made here, the shop still followed the tradition of Rue Cler merchants who worked and lived in their stalls as well.

10. Oldest Building and Charcuterie-Traiteur Jeusselin

On Rue Cler, the oldest building, located at #37, has two gable windows on its roof and dates back to the early 1800s, when this street was a suburban village in Paris. Today on the ground floor is Charcuterie-Traiteur Jeusselin, which makes delicious food for you to take with you if you want. For many years now, Parisians have been taking advantage of such establishments as a source of ready-prepared side dishes for their homemade main courses because of their small-sized kitchens.

A specialty of charcuteries is pork products like sausages, pâté, and ham, and the competition is fierce amongst them. The diplomas and awards showcased by Jeusselin underscore its quality workmanship. Many charcuteries have extended their operations to include traiteurs who are also involved in selling takeaway foods that could be pre-ordered or bought off-the-shelf, while others also offer pastries and wines, among other things. As far as their plats du jour are concerned, Davoli, directly opposite it, competes intensely with Jeusselin.

Both shops show their best wares before lunchtime and dinnertime each day. If you feel like a roast chicken, get one hot from 11:00 AM or after 5:00 PM when Parisians buy food items for picnics on summer days. It's a simple process: order your meal, take your ticket to the cashier's desk, where you pay, and then return with a receipt in hand to collect your food.

Next door to Jeusselin is Glacier Artisan Martine Lambert, which some consider to have the best ice cream in Paris (Street Food Guy). Just beyond there...

11. Café du Marché and More

Café du Marché on the corner provides an ideal vantage point from which to watch life along the busy street (see detailed info here). This café is like the living room of Rue Cler, where neighbors meet before retiring home and often eat well but inexpensively. The owner recognized this by pricing his menu low so that those who live nearby could afford to eat out five nights each week. For a budget-friendly meal, grab a seat and check the chalkboard for the plat du jour. Also, note how non-smoking laws have made outside seating popular.

Across from Rue Cler is the Aldi grocery store, which is quite sterile and bulk-focused, not unlike Costco. However, few locals visit it due to the lack of space in most Parisian apartments. The latest trend involves ordering non-perishables online, purchasing fruits three times a week, and fresh bread daily. Hence, it has surpassed Rue Cler's usual strict building permit design guidelines, as seen in its modern façade.

Turn right at Café du Marché and walk two doors down Rue du Champ de Mars toward...

12. L'Epicerie Fine

This fine-foods boutique has very nice owners, Pascal and Nathalie, who want to make tourists aware of French culinary passion through easy English translation. They also offer Berthillon ice cream as well as gourmet treats such as caramel, balsamic vinegar, or olive oil, be it French or Italian-made.

When crossing back to Rue Cler, one will often see a line of locals waiting at a bakery on the corner for their day-to-day baguette supply.

13. Artisan Boulangerie

The price of an ordinary loaf of bread has been regulated by the government since the French Revolution. For a bakery to be called a boulangerie, it must bake its bread in-house under the law. Different locals prefer well-baked or middling-doughy baguettes to other types available at Paris' numerous boulangeries. They say that one cannot be good at both bread and pastry, yet this trend is not observed by the baker in Artisan Boulangerie, which excels in both specialties, much to the satisfaction of Rue Cler habitués.

14. Mephisto Shoe Store

Just a little way down is the Mephisto Shoe Store. These shoe stores are as popular with pedestrians as those selling pastries in this fashion-conscious city. (French-made Mephistos are less expensive here than they are in the United States.) This is because many people do not own cars in a city where quality shoes are indispensable. For instance, Parisians can often be seen walking from their apartments to lunch hour, shops, and Métro stations—sometimes more than two flights up.

15. Cler Fleurs and Butcher Shop

Across the street is Cler Fleurs. Because most central Parisians live in apartments or condos without yards or gardens, they spend heavily on indoor plants and fresh flowers. There are usually balcony flower boxes; this limited space comes alive with colorful blooms during the warmer months.

A few doors away is a butcher shop that offers insight into traditional French meat consumption habits. Be sure to check out its chalkboard, where various cuts of beef (boeuf), veal (veau), pork (porc), and lamb (agneau) are written up for sale. This type of butchery is losing favor among young French people who consider it an unimportant occupation; however, its presence remains powerful on Rue Cler.

16. City Info Post

There's an electronic signpost (10 feet up) at the end of Rue Cler where it meets a busier street, which directs people to local information websites such as transport updates, questionnaires, job opportunities, and community events. Take note of the huge glass recycling container and see-through garbage bags close by. Over several years in the 1990s, Paris experienced instances of bin bombings whereby camp stove canisters rigged up in metal bins exploded to produce lethal flying objects. They have since fitted translucent bags as a solution.

Across Avenue de la Motte-Picquet is a tabac.

17. Tabac, La Cave à Cigares

In France, adults over 18 can only buy tobacco from tobacconists (called tabacs), which are similar to liquor stores in America. The European Union regulations also require cigarette packages to carry graphic images that cover about half their area with the words fumer tue (smoking kills).

Tabacs serve as neighborhood cash desks, selling stamps and sometimes public transit tickets. "LOTO" is a popular lottery that brings considerable revenue into the government's coffers. An opportunity for US smokers could be presented by a petit Habana cigar—who would pass on buying an excellent Cuban stogie?

18. Pharmacy

Next door, there is an appropriate pharmacy for this location. In France, when one falls lightly ill, he or she usually goes first to the pharmacist, who can diagnose them and prescribe medicines.

The Conclusion of Your Walk.

If you pick up picnic items on this walk, there are two wonderful places to have them: Go left onto Avenue de la Motte-Picquet from Rue Cler and find a small park near the Army Museum (cross Boulevard de la Tour Maubourg). Alternatively, turn right and go to Champ de Mars Park, and from there to the Eiffel Tower. If you are ready to move forward with your trip, the Ecole Militaire Metro stop is just down Avenue de la Motte-Picquet on the right.

THE ROYAL PALACE OF VERSAILLES

Versailles, which means "look at this," was the last royal vision of grandeur in France and was the cultural capital of Europe for nearly one hundred years. The influence of Versailles' court under Louis XIV determined European culture, which is still observed today.

Versailles has three main attractions to see. Notably, the Château—the central palace—has luxurious apartments adorned with chandeliers that once housed French royalty. It features statues and fountains, as well as meticulously landscaped pathways within its sprawling grounds. Another example is the Trianon Palaces and Domaine de Marie-Antoinette, a rustic hideaway consisting of small, fascinating palaces, including Marie's heartbreaking Hamlet.

Important Information

Cost and Reservations: When it comes to gaining access to the Château, timed-entry tickets are necessary. Prior booking can be done through the Versailles website free of charge. Tickets can also be bought at Paris Tourist Information Centers or FNAC department stores (for a small fee). You may consult the "Using the Paris Museum Pass" part to learn about where you can go if you have a pass.

Château: €18 (Château only) or €20 for a Le Passeport ticket (which includes Trianon/Domaine; €27 on Garden Spectacle days) is what you will spend upon entry into either attraction; all fees include an audioguide and are waived on the first Sunday from November until March. Trianon Palaces and Domaine de Marie-Antoinette: Entry costs 12€, except for every first Sunday of November through March, when it costs nothing.

Gardens: Open every day during the working week between April and October but closed during special events (usually on Tuesday, Friday, Saturday, and Sunday in high season—see "Spectacles in the Gardens" later). Starting from November up to March, opening times are adjusted to work with the coming night.

Hours: Tuesday through Sunday from 9:00 to 18:30, and from November to March, open until 17:30, closed on Mondays. Tuesday through Sunday from 12:00 to 18:30, and from November to March, open until 17:30, closed on Mondays. The last entry is forty-five minutes before closing time. Gardens are open every day between eight o'clock in the morning and half past eight in the evening; they close at six p.m., however, during the winter months.

Getting There: Versailles is a 35-minute train ride southwest of Paris. Take RER/Train-C either from Gare d'Austerlitz, St.-Michel, Musée d'Orsay, Invalides, Pont de l'Alma, or Champ de Mars. For example, buy a four-zone all-day Easy Pass Navigo Découverte or get a round-trip ticket up to Versailles Rive Gauche/Château (around €7.20 round-trip). Look at the departure board for the next "Versailles Rive Gauche/Château" train and its platform number. On exiting the station, take a right, then a left, into First Boulevard, and march along it for about ten minutes till you get there.

Using the Paris Museum Pass: All places except Gardens in case of Spectacle Days, such as Château as well as Trianon/Domaine, receive this card freely but require a reservation of a time slot ("Palace ticket") on the Versailles website.

Buying Tickets in Versailles: Without any prepaid tickets or passes, you may have to wait in long lines at the Château entrance gate. If you can connect to the internet, first check out websites for availability, especially if they're accessible online. Tickets can be obtained near the train station at the Versailles Tourist Information Office, and sometimes there is space for guided tours (€55, across from the train station at #10) listed on Get Your Guide. As a last resort, visit the crowded Château ticket office to your left of the palace entrance.

Crowd-Beating Strategies: Avoid holidays, Sundays, Tuesdays, and Saturdays during high season—Thursdays and Fridays are best. In the Château's courtyard (10:00–12:00 longest lines) and at the entrance, there are two security checkpoints.

Planning Your Time: By 8:00, start leaving Paris to beat queues by lining up before the palace opens at 9:00. After that, a self-guided tour of the Château interior is followed by lunch. In the afternoon, visit the Gardens and Trianon Palaces/Domaine de Marie-Antoinette. Save time by not going to Trianon/Domaine, which takes about 1.5 hours plus a 30-minute walk each way.

Tours: This tour is English-guided; it lasts for one hour and thirty minutes in Château with extra rooms included and without standing in line to pass through security (€10). Call or go online (at different places) for bookings.

Spectacles in the Gardens: The Les Grandes Eaux Musicales event features classical music set against fifty-five fountains (€9.50; April-Oct Sat-Sun 11:00-12:00 & 15:30-17:00, also Tue May-June 11:00-12:00 & 14:30-16:30). For some days between April and October, Les Jardins Musicaux is only music without fountains (€8.50).

On Saturday nights in summer, there is Les Grandes Eaux Nocturnes, which gives you a chance to see illuminated groves, flickering pools, and spouting fountains with music accompaniment ending with fireworks at night (€29 on Saturdays early June-mid Sept 20h30–23h fireworks at 22h50).

Eating: Near the Château entrance, the Grand Café d'Orléans provides good-value self-service meals, ideal for picnicking in the Gardens. There are several cafés and snack stands in the gardens, including one near Latona Fountain. The Versailles town center offers excellent selections along Rue de Satory and Place du Marché.

Returning to Paris: From the Versailles Rive Gauche/Château station, catch any departing train back to the city. Taxis for the 30-minute ride (without traffic) cost about €65. Alternatively, take the metro (the yellow Juvisy line) from Versailles Château Rive Gauche (a 6-minute walk from the palace), making 13 stops and getting off at Saint-Michel Notre-Dame.

Versailles Self-Guided Tour Overview

On this self-led walk, we shall tour the Château, the beautiful gardens, and the Trianon Palaces and Domaine de Marie-Antoinette at the end of the garden. Stand in front of the huge courtyard and face the palace; that is where you will find entrance A, which is usually marked with a line.

Original Château and Courtyard

It was originally a hunting lodge for young Louis XIV that started life as a humble château with its clock tower section. The sun king's private chamber (the three arched windows below the clock) faced eastwards to catch the rising sun. The building was arranged on an east-west axis. King Louis XIV later built wings to expand it into the present 'U' shape when he became king and added long northern and southern wings that cost half of France's GNP for one year.

An image of the activity taking place here 300 years ago would have involved up to 5,000 aristocrats attending various events plus their attendants. They traveled in sedan-chair taxis from games to parties to secret rendezvous while messengers ran around delivering messages with roast legs of lamb included! Horse-drawn carriages brought fashionably dressed passengers through ornate gates after traveling from Paris down a wide boulevard. The tourists were joined by pickpockets, palace staff members, and souvenir sellers in this courtyard.

Entering the Château

When you enter Chateau, there is an information desk where you can get maps or check your bags. Cross back through the courtyard, following everyone else into the Palace again. There are various rooms to walk through before reaching our starting point on this tour. Climbing up takes one all along until entering the big room, which has a golden brown color with doorways looking over the royal chapel.

Royal Chapel

The musicians would start to play at 10:00 a.m., and then the large golden doors would open, letting Louis XIV and his family onto the balcony for morning mass. Louis looked down at the golden altar as lower-status nobles kneeled on the ground floor with their backs to the altar, watching him worship God. This place was used for significant religious ceremonies, including the wedding of Marie-Antoinette to Louis XVI.

Versailles, which was built like a vast pagan temple for the glorification of King Louis XIV, has a Royal Chapel that acts as a slight acknowledgment of Christianity. Go into the next room, which has even more opulent interiors, complete with a fireplace and a colorful ceiling painting.

Hercules Drawing Room

Dine in this picturesque Hercules Drawing Room set up for grand suppers, balls, and receptions. In silk gowns, powdered wigs, rouge lips, and artificial beauty spots (that's just for men), couples elegantly danced to string quartet melodies. Opposite this fireplace on the other side of the wall hangs a painting by Paolo Veronese showing Jesus amidst Venetian partying. This picture was much loved by Louis XIV, who had a room designed around it, so everything in it, from columns, arches, and friezes, aligns with painted architecture, giving it the impression as if the picture was an extension of this chamber. The ceiling shows Hercules dashing along in a chariot on their way to his wedding, just like when Louise XIV's daughter got married here.

From here, the tour turns one way, guiding you through King's Wing, starting with a little green room on the ceiling of which there is a pink goddess. Room names usually come from the paintings on their ceilings.

Salon of Overflow

The Salon of Overflow offered refreshments when the party in the Hercules Room got too hot. Silver trays would have liqueurs, coffee, juice, chocolates, and sometimes a three-bean salad. Louis was a good host who liked to relax with his visitors at night. If he liked you, he might take you to his private study through a secret door to show off his collections, including the Mona Lisa painting.

Venus Room

In this Venus room, love reigned supreme. Here, couples played amidst the flowers that were sent down by the deity of love to trap people in love's net. The painted columns at both ends of this room's space make it seem as if it extends into mythical courtyards like those depicted thereon. The image of Louis XIV as a Roman emperor belies his humble beginnings. After being ill-treated by the French parliaments in early Versailles, it turned out to be a pleasure palace as an ultimate revenge for him.

Diana Room

Louis and company used to play billiards while ladies reclined on cushions made out of Persian carpets while music streamed from an adjacent room in Diana's chamber, which served as an excellent resting place for them. It was hard for him to lose due to his royal status; however, Louis was a sore loser since he was a great pool player. In the middle are Giovanni Lorenzo Bernini's famous busts, showing a 27-year-old Louis XIV looking very handsome and dashing with a windblown cloak and hair looking straight ahead. Like most kings do, Louis did not shy away from enjoying life—hunting during the day (as shown by Diana Huntress on the ceiling) and romantic escapades at night.

Games were more than just fun; rather, they were critical components of Louis' domestication of the nobility, a political strategy. He ruled without interference by keeping the aristocracy preoccupied with courtly pleasures. A popular pastime was gambling, which often involved a card game similar to blackjack. The losers would be lent money by Louis, who in turn controlled them.

Mars Room

Another name for this room is Guard Room, and it used to belong to the Swiss bodyguards of Louis. On its ceiling, there is Mars, the god of war, riding a chariot pulled by wolves in what is usually considered a red room. Despite not being original, most of the furniture here belongs to that period, thereby maintaining a historical ambiance.

Mercury Room

Louis XIV himself was an artist, and Versailles served as his canvas. This might have been Louis' official (but not real) bedroom, where he would ceremonially rise every morning as Sun King just to keep his subjects. From such a four-poster bed like the one from 18th-century showrooms today, you will get up in the morning, dress up, and sit down for prayers while nobles around are amazed at your clean mind, piousness, and dignity. Over breakfast, they may be entertained by watching him deftly chop off an eggshell top or, after dinner, scramble to hold his chamber candle when he has slipped into royal night clothes.

Apollo Room

The Apollo Room was the grand hall that Louis XIV used as his courtroom. He sat atop a high platform on a 10-foot-tall golden and silver canopy throne. Every detail of this room declares the glory of Louis XIV. The ceiling is painted with Apollo dragging the sun across the sky and giving warmth to America. It shows an Indian girl guarding her eggs from a crocodile. Above the fireplace, there is the famous Hyacinthe Rigaud's portrait of Louis XIV at 63 years old, which details plenty of legs on him for somebody who doesn't know about dancing. Evening parties were held in this room, where people would dance around the throne.

Louis had over three hundred wig collections in his possession, making him a fashion icon not only in Europe but also in America. Almost godlike reverence was given to Louis XIV while his subjects idolized him as their ideal man—the true embodiment of Renaissance man itself.

War Chamber

The War Room is a visual representation of Louis XIV's obsession with war; it is adorned in marble, gilding, stucco, and paint. Lady of France on the ceiling, who hurls thunderbolts to smite foes. A relief on the wall shows Louis XIV triumphant on a horse over his fallen enemies. But his greatest accomplishment was to be done in the next room, the Hall of Mirrors.

Mirrors Hall

When it was opened, the splendor of the hall was unprecedented. In those days, mirrors were luxury items, and they were huge in numbers as well as size. It is nearly 250 feet long, with seventeen arched mirrors facing seventeen windows that offer fabulous views of the gardens. The hall has twenty-four gilded candelabras, eight Roman emperors' busts, and eight classical-style statues (seven ancient). Although he remains dominant at the center panel most of the time, he appears in other places too.

Imagine this vast area lit with thousands of candles and teeming with ambassadors, nobles, and gentlemen in brocade coats and powdered wigs. At the far end sat the king on his temporary throne, which had been shifted from the Apollo Room temporarily. While an orchestra played, servants carried trays filled with canapés made of silver past them along its glaring floorboards. The era is reflected in these mirrors, where people no longer felt guilty for vanity or taking pleasure in fine appearances but rather indulged themselves through their looks: laughing, dancing, eating sumptuous food washed down by wine or spirits, and making love at sunset across an extensive canal.

From this point at Versailles' core, you get an idea of its epic proportions. There is nothing like Versailles—the grand palace designed by architect Louis Le Vau; the intricacy provided by Charles

Le Brun inside; plus André Le Nôtre's colossal gardens surrounding it all. To some extent, this may also be seen as the place where the Treaty of Versailles was signed by Germany and the Allies in 1919 to end World War I, thus setting the stage for World War II.

To find the door that leads into the palace's central part, one needs to go back a few stations.

King's Chambers and Meeting Rooms

To enter room number one (a large one), walk through it, and you will be at Louis XIV's luxurious bedroom, complete with an impressive bed and balustrade. The room decoration varied from season to season. This little room is exactly at the center of the vast horseshoe-shaped palace; it opens onto its inner courtyard and faces east to see dawn. It was intended as a seat of power in France. Picture this poignant moment in 1789 when here stood Louis XVI, great-great-great-grandson of Louie XIV, forced to face angry crowds clamoring to end divine monarchy.

Go back again to the Hall of Mirrors and reach its very end while enjoying beautiful views across the garden. Then proceed...

Peace Room

Louis XIV grew tired of war by the time his very long rule ended. This follow-up on War Room depicts Germany, Holland, and Spain receiving peace as cupids play with abandoned cannons and swords turn into violins. He once advised his great-grandson to "be a peaceful king," which seemed to be headed by him. The oval painting over the fireplace shows a 19-year-old Louis XV presenting Europe with an olive branch wherever such a painting is displayed above fireplaces.

Salon des Nobles

In this pale green room, the queen of Louis XV and her entourage conversed on politics. They also talked about food, rumors, literature, the arts, fashion, and even philosophy. Each one of these three kings was an enlightened monarch who supported the arts as well as progress. These conversations became the genesis for liberal thought, which ended up leading to revolution.

Queen's Antechamber

This was the grand Couvert or dining place for public royalty. A typical lunch would feature four various soups, two whole truffled birds, lamb meat, and some slices of ham, followed by fruits and pastries together with compotes and jams. One such painting could be that of Marie-Antoinette, who is famous for her glamorous living style; it was a piece intended to change her public image in which she appeared with three children.

Queen's Guard Room

It is possible that they were enraged by the fashionable tastes in a wallpaper of the queen on October 5th, 1789. It was from this room that a group rushed into where Marie-Antoinette hid herself and overpowered her guards before taking her off along with her husband. Thereafter, those angry peasants looted the palace in revenge for years of starvation and oppression. The stripped-out palace was refurnished again ten years later, but today it can be seen as a national museum.

Coronation Room

Soon after getting rid of their king, the French crowned another emperor. This room was built during the Napoleonic era when Napoleon Bonaparte sailed across most parts of Europe. In the huge painting, we witness him crowning himself as emperor over a newly revived "Roman" Empire (the original now hangs in the Louvre). Here you can notice a young, charming Napoleon in 1796 if you look at the window; next to him, there is a portrait dating from later decades showing an ever less revolutionary person looking more like a monarch.

Now we have reached Château's end. Ascend down the stairs to take a rest in the Salon de Thé Angelina. Finally, go downstairs further and leave the palace, then turn right into Les Jardins (gardens) at the back of the château.

The Sun King Louis XIV was a proponent of the divine right of kings and demonstrated his absolute power by behaving like a god over them. The King's total domination is revealed by these magnificent gardens, so intricately planned, trimmed, and decorated. The Garden is large. For some people, walking leisurely around the well-manicured bushes surrounding the chateau and quickly peeping at Royal Drive is enough. However, even if you don't proceed to Trianon/Domaine area a little walk down to Apollo Basin (ten minutes on foot), straight back through the same road will be worth it.

Come into the Gardens until you reach a staircase that overlooks everything from the top step. Turn your back on...

View Down the Royal Drive

I think that this is Versailles' most awe-inspiring spot. As you stand in front of the palace, there's no boundary to this land. Versailles was created along an eight-mile axis, including its grounds as well as the town itself, marking one of the earliest examples of urban planning since Roman times and a model for future capitals such as Washington, DC, or Brasiia.'"Then look down at Royal Drive and see the Apollo Fountain roundabout, ahead of which is the Grand Canal." On either side of 'Royal Drive' were groves planted with trees brought from various parts of the world, arranged in geometrical order, and studded with statues and fountains. Of these, 300 are still available out of the original 1500 fountains.

Go down the steps until a close-up view reveals frogs and lizards on…

Latona Basin

This circular fountain tells a story about the birth of Apollo and his sister Diana. Atop it are Apollo and Diana as children, with their mother Latona facing the Apollo Fountain. Insulted by local villagers because she got pregnant before marriage, Zeus turned them into frogs and lizards; hence, they do exist in abundance here." As you walk, "there are ancient" statues made by 17th-century French sculptors. Find the Colonnade, hidden in the woods on the left side of the Royal Drive, about three-quarters of the way to the Apollo Basin…

How to Get Around the Gardens

On Foot: From the castle, you can walk down to the Grand Canal and go past two Trianon palaces. Beyond those is Domaine de Marie-Antoinette, where at its farthest end is Hamlet. The total walking time will range between 45 and 60 minutes, including sightseeing.

By Bike: There is a bike rented by the Grand Canal for €9 an hour or E20 for a half day, open every day from 10 a.m. to 6 p.m. Although bicycles are not allowed within the premises of Trianon/Domaine, one can be left just around.

By Petit Train: A tram moving slowly from behind Chateau does not allow passengers to alight until it has gone round only once, covering part of the Grand Canal through Petit and Grand Trianons (it costs €8.50 round-trip, €4.60 one-way, and operates 2-4 times per hour, Tue-Sun 11:30–19:00, Mon 11:00–17:00, or with shorter hours in winter).

By Golf Cart: Drive through gardens with golf carts (not allowed inside Trianon/Domaine) following a fixed path only (€38 per hour, then €9 per quarter hour more for up to four persons). You'll find rental stations next to it, as well as behind Chateau on the way into the gardens by the canal.

Colonnade

Instead of prestigious ancient ruins, he built his own. It is made out of a hundred-foot-diameter ring consisting of sixty-four columns made of red marble that support white arches. They would sit in this colonnade and have picnics while listening to string quartets playing classical music, trying to replicate how they felt they were part of Rome.

Apollo Basin

Among all the waterworks at Versailles, fountains used to bring the most fame; this one was its central attraction, with Louis XIV appearing as the sun god driving his radiant chariot across the sky. The half-submerged horses create the illusion of the sun rising from a morning mist when the fountains play. Gravity is used to supply water for all, including smaller ones with underground streams (pumped up by the Seine River) that rise high through their pipes.

The Apollo Basin: When the sun god rises up from the mist when the fountains play. Looking back at this point towards the palace, you realize that what you've walked so far is but a fraction of this immense compound of buildings, gardens, and waterways. People must be grateful they do not have to mow the grass.

Grand Canal

This was as close as anyone could get to having a Venetian experience before virtual reality. Gondoliers carried couples over these waters to "O Sole Mio," played by barge orchestras. The canal stretches one mile long.

Next stop: Trianon Palaces and Domaine de Marie-Antoinette, an isolated part of the gardens that's accessible only upon purchasing a ticket.

Trianon Palaces and Domaine de Marie-Antoinette

Versailles was initially designed to provide an escape from the strains of kingship. However, it soon became as busy as Paris itself. To get away even further, however, Louis XIV built a smaller palace in the countryside. His successors moved even farther from the Château and French politics, creating an ideal haven called Marie Antoinette's Domaine, with palaces, ponds, pavilions, and pleasure gardens.

The Grand Trianon

The Grand Trianon, nestled among gardens delicate and pink, is a perfect summer residence. This was the king's private residence, away from his main palace. Often, Louis XIV spent a few nights here each week, close to this little village of Trianon. The rooms inside are decorated with various types of furniture that belonged to different rulers, like kings, dauphins, and nobles, during different periods in history. For instance, Louis XIV alone had three separate bedrooms in Versailles for himself throughout his life span; this study aims to examine the eras of Louis XIV (1688–1715) and Napoleon Bonaparte (1810–1814).

The Mirrors Salon (Room 2), spacious yet bright, still retains its original white walls furnished with mirrors belonging to Louis XIV, accompanied by Empire-style pieces owned by Napoleon. Imagine waking up on a beautiful sunny morning in Room 3: The Bedroom of Empress Maria Feodorovna, throwing open curtains and looking straight out onto some well-kept gardens. You can go outside through this open-air colonnade (Peristyle), which connects two wings. Previously, there were windows in this pink-columned corridor so that one could enjoy garden vistas even during rain.

The Emperor's Family Drawing Room used to be the theater for Luis IV and the game room for Luis XV, but it also served as a family room in the case of Napoleon. After Napoleon's defeat, King Louis-Philippe I resided here while he was the king. You can then proceed through some other rooms to get to Napoleon's living room, Room 11, which is known as the Malachite Room because of its decorative green basin, vases, and candelabras made from Russian malachite that were presented to him by Czar Alexander I.

Move clockwise around the Grand Trianon to reach the French Pavilion next. Continue towards the Petit Trianon by following signs and crossing a footbridge over...

French Pavilion

This small building (usually closed), cream-colored, has several rooms opening outward with large French windows to let in fresh air. The summer evenings were spent here at nightfall by Marie Antoinette, together with her family and friends, enjoying music, parlor games, and a sweet life. Beyond lies the Petit Trianon palace; it is a large square structure with lines... Turn left halfway there for a view of...

Marie-Antoinette's Theater

It was designed for a select few who could go inside it and watch Marie Antoinette act in the plushness of this dollhouse theater with 100 seats. It is situated not far from Petit Trianon; hence, before you arrive at this place, visit...

Belvedere, Rock, and Grotto

The octagon-shaped Belvedere palace has more windows than walls. It had open doors that served as the stage for musicians playing serenades for nobles. On the left-hand side, one sees Belvedere "Rock," an artificial mountain sloping down into a pond with water cascades, while on the right-hand is a hidden Grotto. Turn east toward Belvedere (as if looking straight at it). Cross a little stream going from the pond until you see a round, funny tower surrounded by shingles houses on one side and half-timbered cottages on the other. Walk up there and find yourself inside a...

Hamlet

Marie Antoinette longed for the idyllic life of a peasant—not that lived by real peasants, but the fairytale one with simple country pleasures. It is the main building, consisting of two buildings connected by a wooden skywalk. Besides a billiard room, library, elegant dining hall, and 2 living rooms included in it (different from a usual farmhouse that has a billiard room, library, and sitting hall together), Hamlet was a working farm that had a dairy (close to the lighthouse tower), a water mill, a pigeon coop, as well as domestic animals. Walk beyond the lighthouse tower to see where cows, goats, chickens, and ducks were kept by the queen's servants.

Return to the Petit Trianon, where you will spot the white dome of the...

Petit Trianon

Constructed by Louis XV for his mistress, Madame de Pompadour, as a private retreat, he later gave it as a present to his next mistress, Countess du Barry. This was the place Marie-Antoinette called home after ascending to the throne when Louis XVI ascended it. This is so because she found politics at court in the main Château overwhelming. As you explore this palace, you'll get to see some portraits and other things related to these great characters. Don't forget that she had a small bathroom with an advanced (for those days) hole-in-a-wooden-plank toilet.

Marie-Antoinette made it her sanctuary. On its lawn, she constructed a merry-go-round. Contrary to her bad image in public, Marie-Antoinette was a nice girl from Vienna who couldn't fit in with Versailles' elite. Marie-Antoinette needed an escape from all this and to recreate the warm and homely lifestyle of her childhood. She sought comfort here while Parisian cafés plotted against the ancien régime.

It takes thirty minutes to walk southeast from the exit (plus ten more minutes if on foot to reach the train station) to return to the main Chateau. Instead, there is also a petit train from just outside the Petit Trianon's wall that goes back towards Château. For those following the "Versailles" map that had been given earlier in this chapter, they can have a slightly shorter walk towards the train station through downtown Versailles.

Paris has world-famous museums like the Louvre and Orsay; famous sights like the Eiffel Tower or Arc de Triomphe; wide boulevards; ancient churches; and modern buildings. More than one visit can allow you to visit all the places mentioned above. This guidebook focuses on key attractions in the City of Light to make your trip more enjoyable.

These listed attractions are arranged into walkable districts to save visitors time. Besides, how to avoid queuing and where to eat out nearby are also included...

ADVANCE TICKETS AND SIGHTSEEING PASSES

Online ticket sales at no additional cost are available for most major tourist attractions in Paris. Online tickets must be purchased in advance for the Louvre, the Orangerie, the Sainte-Chapelle, and Versailles. Although it is not obligatory to buy prior tickets for going to see the Eiffel Tower, Catacombs, or Conciergerie, it is reasonable to do so as they are likely to be full, especially in the summer.

However, this does not mean that you must wait for a presale notification before buying them (although you will still have to go through security). Drinking water regularly should always be encouraged. This can be done along with using the Paris Museum Pass discussed below, which will save both time and money.

Book Tickets Ahead

Save your digital copy by purchasing your tickets online, either by phone or via email, and then avoid all queues when you get there. Only book directly from their official website. The process may involve registering an account and several steps, but it helps evade third-party charges. If you have a Paris Museum Pass and would like to book a visit that it covers, use the passholder option to book free admission time by inputting your Museum Pass number. An email will usually follow that comes along with a QR code, which serves as your digital ticket when printed out. On arrival, look for the "ticket holders" line (avec billet).

Paris Museum Passes

The Louvre Museum is one of the several major sites covered by the Paris Museum Pass, along with Orsay, Sainte-Chapelle, and Versailles, among others. However, other places such as Montparnasse Tower, Marmottan Museum, Opéra Garnier, Catacombs, and Eiffel Tower are not covered under this pass. The pass lasts two days consecutively: 52 euros; four days: 66 euros; six days: 78 euros (no discounts for youth or seniors). For example, if one goes through the Louvre, Orsay, Sainte-Chapelle, and Rodin Museum over two days—the first four entrances—the pass 'pays for itself' quickly.

More information about the Paris Museum Pass can be found here. In Paris, it is sold at museums, monuments, tourist information centers (TIs), and some gift stores near major attractions. One should avoid purchasing it at major museums like the Louvre since there are possibilities of long lines and stock-outs.

However, it's important to note that even with this pass, you still have to reserve free timed admissions online for such sites as The Louvre. It should be planned very well to use the pass in a maximized way. Only pick it up when you are ready to visit covered attractions within continuous days. Some of these places are closed either on Mondays or Tuesdays, so one should check their operational days.

Last Ticketing Tips

If there is no online booking for your desired date, think about buying "coupe-file" (line-skipping) tickets from third-party suppliers, usually at an added cost. Such tickets could be purchased from TIs, FNAC departmental chains, and other travel agencies similar to Paris Webservices and Fat Tire Tours.

Notre Dame Cathedral

This cathedral, which is 850 years old and has a rich history, was ravaged by a catastrophic fire in 2019. The inside and parts of its vicinity will remain closed for many years, but you can still admire the grandeur of its exterior. See the Historical Walks in Paris chapter.

Sainte-Chapelle

This little Gothic church, famous for being home to Europe's finest stained-glass windows, shines with a myriad of colors.

Riverside Promenades and Paris Plages

Paris has converted some sections of the riverbank into car-free zones for walking, cycling, eating out, and family outings. For instance, one section runs along the Left Bank near Pont de l'Alma (in front of the Eiffel Tower) and the Orsay Museum, while another stretches from the Louvre to Place de la Bastille on the right bank. Every summer, a one-mile stretch of the Right Bank turns into faux beaches called Paris Plages, with numerous activities taking place here.

Paris Archaeological Crypt

Discover Roman remains such as medieval village layouts and the early stages of development in Paris. These ruins have an intriguing mix of foundations from diverse periods, like the ancient rampart, the oldest preserved wall ever found in town, a medieval road, or a Roman building that had an underfloor heating system. Multimedia displays help to make sense of all this mess. €8 covered by Museum Pass; Tue-Sun: 10 a.m.–6 p.m.; closed Monday; excellent audioguide €5 entrance right front of the cathedral, +33 1 55 42 50 10.

Conciergerie

One-time prison for Marie-Antoinette and many others on their way to Guillotine offers an exhibit space with good English explanations about its history and inmates' lives there. €11.50 timed-entry ticket; €18.50 combo-ticket with Sainte-Chapelle; covered by Museum Pass; daily 9:30-18:00, multimedia guide €5, 2 Boulevard du Palais, Mo: Cité, +33 1 53 40 60 80.

Deportation Memorial

Go down the steps and experience the sad tribute to the French victims (over two hundred thousand dead) of Nazi concentration camps.

Major Museums Neighborhood

Louvre

Europe's oldest, largest, most renowned, and second-most-crowded museum (after the Vatican), the Louvre houses the Mona Lisa, Venus de Milo, and countless other masterpieces of Western art.

Orangerie Museum

The Orangerie is a gem, showcasing select works by Claude Monet and his contemporaries. Begin with the museum's highlight: Monet's Water Lilies. These eight enormous, curved panels immerse you in Monet's

130

garden at Giverny. He designed a special studio with skylights and wheeled easels to create these masterpieces, which some consider the first "art installation"—art displayed in a space specifically designed to enhance the viewer's experience. The scenes depict Monet's garden pond, adorned with water lilies and reflections of the sky, clouds, and trees.

Downstairs features works bridging the Impressionist and Modernist eras, including Utrillo, Cézanne, Renoir, Matisse, and Picasso, providing a snapshot of early 20th-century art. €12.50 for timed-entry ticket—reserve online, free on the first Sunday of the month; €18 combo ticket with Orsay Museum; inquire about combo ticket with Monet's garden and the tiny house in the Giverny, hedged by Museum Pass; Wed-Mon from 9:00–18:00, closed Tue; audioguide: €5, English guided tours: €6, in Tuileries Garden near Place de la Concorde (Mo: Concorde); +33 1 44 77 80 07; www.musee-orangerie.fr.

Army Museum and Napoleon's Tomb

Situated in the Les Invalides complex—a veterans' hospital built by Louis XIV—this site features Napoleon's tomb and Europe's premier military museum. Witness the history of warfare, from stone axes to the Axis powers. Napoleon Bonaparte lies majestically under a grand dome at its center, a poignant pilgrimage for history enthusiasts. The museum showcases medieval armor, cannons, muskets, Louis XIV-era uniforms, weapons, and even Napoleon's mounted horse. The most captivating section covers the two World Wars, presenting a chronological journey through World War I trench warfare, France's losses, the Treaty of Versailles, World War II, and the eventual Allied victory, with special emphasis on the French Resistance and Charles de Gaulle's pivotal role. €14, covered by Museum Pass; daily 10:00–18:00, Napoleon's Tomb open until 21:00 on Tue; multimedia guide:

€5; 129 Rue de Grenelle, Mo: La Tour Maubourg, Varenne, or Invalides; +33 1 44 42 38 77.

⭐ ⭐ Rodin Museum

This accessible museum with gardens showcases the passionate works of Auguste Rodin (1840–1917), the greatest sculptor since Michelangelo. Highlights include The Kiss, The Thinker, The Gates of Hell, and more, all beautifully displayed in the mansion where Rodin lived and worked. Rodin's sculptures reveal deep emotions through their epic, dynamic human figures. Like Michelangelo's unfinished works, Rodin's statues emerge from raw stone, driven by a life force. These sculptures, with missing limbs and scarred surfaces, elevate imperfection to nobility. Rodin's figures are always in motion, even The Thinker, who, though solidly seated, appears lost in thought. Exhibits trace Rodin's artistic development, explain bronze casting, and show studies leading up to his unfinished masterpiece, The Gates of Hell. Learn about Rodin's tumultuous relationship with his apprentice and lover, Camille Claudel. Reflect on what makes his sculptures so evocative and stroll through the beautiful gardens, which feature many of his greatest works. €13, free first Sun of the month Oct-March, €24 combo-ticket with Orsay Museum, covered by Museum Pass; Tue-Sun 10:00-18:30, closed Mon, Oct-March garden closes at dusk; audio guide: €6, 77 Rue de Varenne, Mo.: Varenne, +33 1 44 18 61 10.

The Eiffel Tower and Nearby

 Eiffel Tower

This iconic 1,063-foot structure, originally built as a tourist attraction, remains a must-see landmark in Paris.

Cathedral of Notre-Dame

This 850-year-old cathedral, rich in history, is recovering from a devastating fire in 2019. The interior and some surrounding areas will be closed for several years, but you can still appreciate its monumental exterior. See the chapter on Historical Walks in Paris.

Sainte-Chapelle

This small Gothic church, renowned for Europe's finest stained glass, glows with color and light.

Rue Cler

This lively market street offers a glimpse into a traditional Parisian neighborhood, showcasing a thriving local culture amidst the city's constant evolution.

Marmottan Museum

This private and less-tourist museum hosts the most extensive collection of Claude Monet's works. Trace Monet's journey through over a hundred pieces, from early sketches to the famous Impression: Sunrise, the painting that launched the Impressionist movement. Enjoy large-scale canvases depicting the water lilies from his Giverny garden. The museum also boasts a remarkable collection of works by Berthe Morisot and other Impressionists, along with an eclectic mix of artifacts, including furniture and illuminated manuscripts. €12, not included in the Museum Pass; inquire about combo tickets with Monet's garden and house at Giverny; Tue-Sun 10:00-18:00, Thu until 21:00, closed Mon; audioguide: €4, 2 Rue Louis-Boilly, Mo: La Muette, +33 1 44 96 50 33, www.marmottan.fr.

Paris Archaeological Crypt

Explore Roman ruins, trace the layout of the medieval village, and see how early Paris developed. The ruins are a fascinating mix of foundations from various periods, including the city's oldest rampart, a medieval road, and a Roman building with a heated floor. Multimedia displays help make sense of it all. €8, covered by Museum Pass, Tue-Sun 10:00-18:00, closed Mon, excellent audioguide, €5, entrance 100 yards in front of the cathedral, +33 1 55 42 50 10.

Conciergerie

Once the prison of Marie-Antoinette and many others en route to the guillotine, this historic building features exhibits with excellent English descriptions, detailing its history and the lives of its prisoners. €11.50 for a timed-entry ticket, €18.50 combo-ticket with Sainte-Chapelle, hedged by Museum Pass, opened Mon-Sun 9:30-18:00, plus audio guide: €5, at 2 Boulevard du Palais, Mo: Cité, +33 1 53 40 60 80.

Deportation Memorial

Descend the steps to experience a somber tribute to the 200,000 French victims of Nazi concentration camps.

Paris Sewer Museum

Explore what happens after you flush. This quick, intriguing, and slightly odorous visit takes you through a few hundred yards of tunnels in the world's first underground sewer system. Learn about the sewer's evolution from Roman times through the medieval period (when waste was washed directly into the river), to Victor Hugo's hero Jean Valjean hiding here in Les Misérables, to today's 1,500 miles of tunnels carrying 317 million gallons of water daily. Essential items include a loaner booklet, map, and audio guide in English (if available). €9, covered by Museum Pass; Tue-Sun 10:00-17:00, closed Mon, last entry one hour before closing; audioguide-€3, located where Pont de l'Alma meets the Left Bank—on the right side of the bridge facing the river, Mo: Alma-Marceau, RER/Train-C: Pont de l'Alma, +33 1 53 68 27 81.

Best Views Over the City of Light

Eiffel Tower: The ultimate Parisian view.

Paris Ferris Wheel: A 200-foot panorama.

Arc de Triomphe: Best when Champs-Élysées shines at night.

Steps of Sacré-Cœur: Climb up or take the funicular to experience the lively atmosphere on the only hill in Paris.

Galeries Lafayette or Printemps: Wonderful sights of the old opera district.

Montparnasse Tower: The only skyscraper in town with a marvelous day view.

Pompidou Center: Great scenes plus contemporary art shows.

Place du Trocadéro: On the ground level, this place offers the best view of the Eiffel Tower.

> **Windo Skybar:** At the Hôtel Hyatt Regency Paris Etoile, a breathtaking 34th-floor bar in an otherwise unremarkable hotel in Paris.

Left Bank

✿ ✿ Cluny Museum (Musée National du Moyen Age)

This treasure trove of medieval art is housed in old Roman baths, showcasing stained glass, Notre Dame carvings, fine goldsmithing, and intricate tapestries. The highlight is the series of six Lady and the Unicorn tapestries, where a noble lady introduces a delighted unicorn to the senses. The enigmatic A Mon Seul Désir tapestry remains a topic of much discussion.

€12, free on the first Sunday of the month, included in the Museum Pass; Tue-Sun 9:30–18:15, closed Mon, last entry 45 minutes before closing; 6 Place Paul Painlevé, Mo: Cluny La Sorbonne, St-Michel, or Odéon; +33 1 53 73 78 10.

✿ The Latin Quarter, Quartier Latin

On the other bank of Notre Dame, its streets were the very heart of Roman Paris. The Latin Quarter is so well-known because it is an artsy and bohemian place. These days, they are lined with cafes that once hosted famous poets and philosophers, such as St. Michel's Boulevard and St. Germain, but are now busy with tourists. Despite being filled with budget eateries, this area retains its youthful and artistic spirit.

✿ Luxembourg Garden

It is like stepping into an Impressionist painting of a 60-acre garden. You can sit near the pond, marvel at flowerbeds that come alive with color every spring, jog around or play tennis or basketball on small courts, glide toy boats, or gaze at people playing chess or puppet shows alike. Situated in Luxembourg Palace, where French Senate meetings take place all the time, this is the perfect venue for watching Parisians at play. Open every day from dawn until dusk. Mon: Odéon, RER/Train-B: Luxembourg.

Catacombs

Go 60 feet below Paris to wander through tunnels containing the skeletons of six million Parisians. To combat overcrowding and sanitation problems in 1785, the city moved remains from church cemeteries into these former limestone quarries. The bones there stand up to five feet high and even as much as eighty feet deep. At the entrance is a sign that says, "Halt! This is the empire of the dead!" Artfully arranged bone line passages and morbid signs lead to bag checks as protection against souvenir thefts before one enters. €29, book online in advance, including audio guide not covered by Museum Pass. Tue-Sun10:00-20:30 closed on Monday €15 same-day tickets may be available online and on-site at 1 Place Denfert-Rochereau, Mo.: Denfert-Rochereau +33 1 43 22 47 63.

St. Sulpice Church

The Grand Orgue at St. Sulpice Church is a must for pipe organ lovers who come from close and far away for the experience of listening to world-class organists with about 300 years of history in this place. This church, which bears a resemblance to St. Paul's Cathedral in London, has a neoclassical facade with two circular towers. Here one finds murals painted by Delacroix as well as a chapel dedicated to Joan of Arc. Organ music can be heard before and after Sunday Mass, followed by a recital given by Daniel Roth Free, daily 7:30–19:30 Mo: St. Sulpice or Mabillon.

Panthéon

This neoclassical monument commemorates French history and serves as the resting place for many national heroes. Go inside and see monuments that depict the struggle of French men and women; there is also a Foucault pendulum showing that our world rotates, while in the crypts you will find people like Rousseau, Voltaire, and Marie Curie, among others. From here, climb up the stairs to the dome observation deck, where you have the opportunity to enjoy both interior and city views. €11.50 per person (included within Museum Pass), €3.50 for entrance into the dome (not covered by Museum Pass); open every day from 10:00–18:30 Oct-March until 18:00 last entry 45 minutes before closing; audioguide: €3 Mo: Cardinal Lemoine +33 1 44 32 18 00.

Montparnasse Tower

Though it may look out of place, this skyscraper has sixty floors providing great views over Paris, which are cheaper than those provided on the Eiffel Tower because it is less crowded. Come early for clear skies and short lines; also, views can be enjoyed from both inside and on the rooftop. Although nighttimes are not as impressive as sunsets, 30% discount (2 people per book), not covered by Museum Pass; daily 10:00-23:30 Oct-March from 11:00 to 22:30; e the entrance is located on Rue de l'Arrivée from the Métro, stay inside the station and follow signs to exit #1. +33 1 45 38 52 56.

Champs-Élysées

One of the most significant streets in Paris and often called the backbone of the city, it is famed for having heavy traffic, but this does not apply on every first Sunday of the month. Though known globally, Champs Elysées has managed to keep its Parisian nature, and a walk down that two-mile boulevard remains a must. It was created by Louis XIV in 1667 and soon became a playground for aristocrats showing off their carriages. By the 1920s, it symbolized luxury with posh residences, grand hotels, and stylish restaurants. Today, this place is occupied by businesses, fashion shops, places where famous people hang out, and many bars.

Start your stroll from Arc de Triomphe, going down along its northern side. Number 116 is "Lido," home to Paris' biggest burlesque cabaret as well as multiplex cinemas. On the opposite side, there is Louis Vuitton's flagship (#101). Uptown French celebrities, mostly film stars, revere Fouquet's café (#99)—watch their names on the pavement nearby or rather have a costly cup of coffee inside if you dare to do so. Ladurée Café (#75) offers takeaway services at an affordable price with some touch of charm still left in it. Continue passing such global brand stores as Sephora, Disney, or Renault till you arrive at the Rond Point intersection (Mo: Franklin D. Roosevelt), or maybe go further towards Place de la Concorde, decorated with an obelisk.

Arc de Triomphe

The monument was ordered by Napoleon to honor his triumph at Austerlitz in 1805; since then, it has been used to commemorate important events like Napoleon's funeral and Germany's occupation during WW2, while receiving Charles de Gaulle back into France victorious after World War II ended there. Take time to scrutinize the intricate carvings with a victorious Napoleon and a zealous Lady Liberty, among others. The flame at the Tomb of the Unknown Soldier is reignited every day at 6:30 p.m.

Climb 284 steps to a viewing platform offering awe-inspiring views from an altitude that makes even traffic below look beautiful for once. It is right in the middle of a grand axis stretching between the Louvre and the modern Grande Arche de la Defense. Look at these 12 streets from above, which join together in a star shape (étoile), with entering cars having priority over those inside; this implies that each comer has to yield to other vehicles on this roundabout. €13 admission includes access to the rooftop; tickets are timed and can be bought online, also free of charge on the first Sundays of November-March (covered by Museum Pass); open daily 10 a.m.–11 p.m., October–Mar till 10:30 p.m. The last entry is made 45 minutes before closing. Place Charles de Gaulle and use the underpass to get there. Mo: Charles de Gaulle-Etoile, +33 1 55 37 73 77.

Petit Palais (and Musée des Beaux-Arts)

On its ground floor, numerous paintings and statues date back from the XVII to XIX centuries, while the downstairs exhibition range covers art pieces starting from ancient Greek antiques through the Art Nouveau era. Among them are Courbet's Sleepers (1866), Monet's Sunset on the Seine at Lavacourt (1880), and works by Mary Cassatt and other Impressionists. Admission free, Tue-Sun: 10 a.m.–6 p.m., Fri until p.m. during special exhibitions except for Mondays; opposite the Grand Palais on Avenue Winston Churchill, Mo.: Champs-Elysées Clemenceau; +33 1 53 43 40 00.

Paris Ferris Wheel (Roue de Paris)

The Paris Ferris Wheel provides a breathtaking view of the city from the north side of the Tuileries Garden, as well as being an attraction at a lively funfair with rides and games for children. It costs €12 per person for two slow revolutions, and each gondola can accommodate two passengers. The wheel is open every day from late June to late August.

Opera Neighborhood

Opéra Garnier

This grand belle époque theater was completed in 1875 for Napoleon III, and it is a wonder. The nicest look from the outside is provided by the Opéra Métro stop, which lets one glimpse the mammoth structure spanning an underground lake that inspired The Phantom of the Opera. Guided tours, self-guided tours with audio guides, or attending a performance will help you get around the interior designed by Charles Garnier. Highlights include the Grand Staircase, chandeliered halls, a 2,000-seat auditorium, and exhibits on opera history. You shouldn't miss Marc Chagall's ceiling and the seven-ton chandelier in the performance hall. Among them are the Fragonard Perfume Museum, Galeries Lafayette, and Café de la Paix. €14 individual ticket (Orsay Museum reduced price to €4 within 8 days of Orsay visit), not covered by Museum Pass; usually daily 10:00-16:15 – mid-July-Aug until 17:15; guided tours in English usually daily at 14:00 can be reserved online, so arrive there at least half an hour early for security check; Mo: Opéra address: 8 Rue Scribe RER/Train-A: Auber,

Check online or at the ticket office (open Mon-Sat 11:30–18:30 and an hour before shows, closed Sun) for performances.

✿ ✿ Jacquemart-André Museum

Although a little worn out, this museum mansion has its charm with an elegant café where visitors can see how art-collecting couple Edouard André and Nélie Jacquemart lived in luxury. There are works by Botticelli, Uccello, Rembrandt, Mantegna, Bellini, and Boucher, as well as Fragonard, to be found in the mansion. The tearoom offers scrumptious cakes and tea. This is a good starting point to walk northward along Rue de Courcelles if one wants to explore Parc Monceau, one of Paris' most beautiful parks. €12 individual ticket (special exhibits surcharge €3-5), not covered by Museum Pass; daily 10:00-18:00 – Mon until 20:30 during special exhibits; buy tickets online in advance (€2 fee) at 158 Boulevard Haussmann Mo: St-Philippe-du-Roule; +33 1 45 62 11 59.

Marais Neighborhood and More

✿ ✿ Carnavalet Museum (Musée Carnavalet)

It is located in a beautiful building and offers an overview of French history, with English explanations to help you make sense of the museum layout. It starts with Louis XIV and finishes with Napoleon and the Belle époque, but the most dramatic section is dedicated to the French Revolution and the 19th century.

The top floor of this museum contains rooms that are devoted to "The French Revolution to the 21st Century," including short historical summaries in each one, which are also written in English. This section is going to tell you about how it all began: God-appointed kings versus unruly crowds, the Bastille as well as decapitated royals, heroes of the Revolution, the Reign of Terror's purges, and finally Napoleon himself.

A curving oak staircase leads up from Paris 1852 to today's series of rooms, showing how modern Paris was created. It begins with Baron Haussmann's renovation of the city at the end of the XIX century and continues up until the Fin de siècle period—the time when can-can dancers used to do their high-kicks at Moulin Rouge, the Eiffel Tower was built, hot air balloons flew above it, belle époque ruled it all, and art nouveau movements emerged along with impressionism.

Free admission; Tue-Sun: 10:00-18:00; closed on Mondays; 16 Rue des Francs Bourgeois; Metro: St-Paul

Montmartre and Sacré-Cœur

On top of this hill stands the Sacré-Cœur Basilica, while Montmartre itself is widely regarded for its bohemian artists and cabaret nightlife. It has attracted painters, poets, and dreamers alike who sought cheap accommodation charges for inexpensive booze and rustic countryside viewable from its pubs or dancehalls, where cancan dancers could be seen performing at night. Today, Montmartre is a mix of attractive clichés, maintaining its village-like atmosphere but teeming with visitors and swindlers during sunny weekends. They come to get a taste of the past, avoid crowded streets, and have a panoramic view over the area, best seen on weekdays or in the early hours of weekend mornings.

Begin your day by stopping at the Sacré-Cœur Basilica. It looks ancient, but it is not, as it was built less than 100 years ago with its striking exterior that features onion domes and pale stone. Inside, you will find impressive mosaics (one being Jesus with his burning heart for mankind), St. Thérèse's statue, a scale model of this church, and stained glass windows devoted to Joan of Arc. For an equally breathtaking view of Paris, climb up 300 steps in a spiral staircase that is 260 feet high.

Just behind the basilica, Montmartre's main square, called Place du Tertre, was once home to Henri de Toulouse-Lautrec and other bohemians, but now it is filled with both tourists and street performers. Montmartre Museum has paintings, posters, photos, music videos, and other things related to cancan-and-cabaret life in the area. And while there, check out the Maurice Utrillo studio.

€14; great audio guide; not included in the museum pass; Open: Wed-Mon: 10:00–18:00; Tue closed; last entry is at least 45 minutes before closing; address: 12 Rue Cortot; phone number: +33 1 49 25 89 39.

Nearby, you can see Moulin de la Galette's famous Renoir painting at the Orsay Museum and the still-functioning Au Lapin Agile cabaret that was located here centuries ago. Picasso's former homes would look rather simple from the outside when you pass by, as would those of Toulouse-Lautrec, Van Gough, and Erik Satie. At the base of this hill, near Métro Blanche, is Moulin Rouge, the best of its kind in Paris, with performances that are both expensive and glamorous. Pigalle is more audacious than the dangerous red-light district of Paris, where it is located.

 Père Lachaise Cemetery

Is a vast necropolis filled with the remains of many famous Parisians, giving an insight into the romantic past of the city. It is as huge and intricate as a small town, and it would be advisable to purchase a cemetery map from one of the florists near the Porte Gambetta entrance. Several graves worth visiting are those of Frédéric Chopin buried in fresh flowers (a Polish pianist), Molière, who was Louis XIV's playwright, Edith Piaf, who had no regrets as a singer, Oscar Wilde, the controversial figure who died in Paris, Jim Morrison (the legendary rock star), Gertrude Stein (an American writer), Héloïse, and Abélard (medieval lovers).

Free entry; open 8:00-18:00 Mon to Fri; opens at 8:30 on Saturdays while Sundays it operates from 9:00 am until winter when it closes at 17:30; located two blocks away from Métro Gambetta but never go to Métro Père Lachaise; +33 1 55 25 82 10.

Pompidou Center

Modern art may not be everyone's cup of tea, but this gallery could house arguably Europe's greatest collection of works produced between the years 1900 and 2000. The site also has temporary exhibitions, another stunning rooftop panorama, and lively street life with performers and crêpe stalls that make it a must-visit destination. The external view displays an exoskeletal design where every pipe duct escalator is seen by all. This architectural decision follows modernist thinking: 'form follows function'.

The permanent collection occupies floors four and five, showcasing artists such as Matisse, Picasso, Chagall, Dali, etc., up to contemporary work. With its innovative style of art that challenges conventional ideas against traditional paintings or sculptures done in previous centuries, Temporary exhibits provide insight into global trends shaping the current art scene.

The ticket price is €14, free on the first Sun of the month; €5 for an escalator to the sixth-floor view (if you don't want to visit the museum); Museum Pass gives admission to the permanent collection plus sixth-floor panoramic views (and some special content); the permanent collection open on Wed-Mon from 11:00 until 21:00, and closed on Tue, the ticket counters close at 20:00; the rest of the building open until 22:00 (Thu until 23:00); avoid crowds by coming after 17:00; Métro Rambuteau or Hôtel de Ville, +33 1 44 78 12 33;

⭐ Exploring the Marais

The Marais is an area with a much more authentic Parisian feel than other touristy neighborhoods because it contains many pre-revolutionary streets and mansions. At a former swamp called Marais in French, which was quite near the king's townhouse located on the fashionable Place des Vosges, hôtels particuliers owned by aristocrats started popping up in the seventeenth century. During and after the Revolution, this district changed into a working-class neighborhood full of artisans and migrants, which became home to Jews who lived in the heart of Paris' Jewish Quarter. Currently, it has become one of the chicest districts, inhabited mainly by young professionals.

To get started exploring from east to west, start with Place de la Bastille (famous for its nightlife) and head west along the bustling Rue Saint-Antoine. Westwards through Rue des Francs-Bourgeois, bordered by fashion boutiques, then turn onto Rue des Rosiers (Jewish area), and Rue Ste. Croix de la Bretonnerie leads there right across Pompidou Center. On Sunday afternoons, shoppers and café-goers make the place lively.

⭐ Place des Vosges

Originally called "Place Royale," this square was built in 1605 by Henry IV and transformed Marais into the most sophisticated neighborhood in Paris. In the middle, there is a statue of Louis XIII, mounted on a horse, that says, "See here what a wonderful square my father made." The place is much-frequented by residents who come here to enjoy the greenness of the park; parents let their children play while they sit side by side on benches or near fountains and watch untidy pigeons hop about with graceful poise under trees. Alongside it are arcades containing cafes and art galleries.

Look at the architecture: Nine buildings on each side, with the two tallest ones at the front and back, which were meant for the king and queen (never used). The red brickwork is sometimes real, sometimes not, topped off with sloping tiled roofs decorated with chimneys and TV aerials—an attractive relic of yesterday.

At 6 Place des Vosges stands Victor Hugo's House, a museum honoring one of France's greatest writers.

Picasso Museum (Musée Picasso)

Regardless of your perception of Picasso as a man, his artistic talent and production in the twentieth century have no equal. This museum changes its collections frequently to provide new shows dedicated to Picasso.

€14 (included in Museum Pass), free on first Sun per month; Tue-Fri 10:30-18:00, Sat-Sun from 9:30 AM; closed Mon, last admission 45 minutes before closing; 5 Rue de Thorigny +33 1 42 71 25 21 Métro: St-Sébastien-Froissart, St-Paul, or Chemin Vert

Jewish Art and History Museum

The museum has an impressive collection of historical objects as well as unique ritual items illustrating Jewish cultural heritage. It focuses on the common culture maintained despite constant dispersion. Travelers will learn about Jewish traditions and observe beautiful clothes and artifacts for daily life and religious purposes. Those familiar with Judaism or who take advantage of the thoughtful audioguide and detailed information will find it particularly rewarding.

€10 includes audioguide (included in Museum Pass), free on first Saturday per month Oct-June; Tue-Fri 11:00-18:00, Sat-Sun from 10:00 AM; extended hours during special exhibitions: – Wed until 9 PM, Sat-Sun till 7 PM; closed Mon throughout the year; last admission 45 minutes before closing time; 71 Rue du Temple +33 1 53 01 86 60 Métro: Rambuteau or Hôtel de Ville, www.mahj.org

Victor Hugo's House

This house located at Place des Vosges was Victor Hugo's house from 1832 to 1848—a towering figure in the French literature scene. It marked his longest stay in one place after The Hunchback of Notre Dame made him famous, and he continued to entertain in Parisian high society here. Go up two floors, which encompass rooms recreating several stages of Hugo's life, starting from his years as a celebrity and ending with his exile, which lasted for nineteen years under Napoleon III's autocratic regime until he turned into a national icon at a later stage of his life. The rooms are full of personal things like family photos and paintings used to illustrate images of Hugo himself, as well as those derived from his works. English texts help provide some historical context about this remarkable writer.

Free for permanent collection (fee for temporary exhibits); Tue–Sun 10 a.m.–6 p.m.; closed Mon; café in the courtyard; good toilets; 6 Place des Vosges; Métro: Bastille St-Paul Chemin Vert, tel. +33 (0)1 42 72 10 16.

Day Trips from Paris

Versailles

Located twelve miles southwest of Paris, the opulent palace and sprawling gardens of Versailles stand as a testament to the grandeur of French royalty.

Chartres: The Town and the Cathedral

An hour southwest of Paris, the charming town of Chartres is home to one of Europe's most magnificent Gothic cathedrals. To visit, catch a train from Paris' Gare Montparnasse (14 trains daily, about €16 one-way). The cathedral is free and open daily from 8:30 to 19:30.

A Page of History

The Beginnings (AD 1–1500)

Julius Caesar successfully conquered the Parisians, thus transforming Paris into a great European city. The French identity emerged from the blending of Latin and Celtic cultures centered on Paris. The Roman city was taken over by Norsemen ("Normans") and then Franks (source of "France"). Charlemagne (768–814), who united the Franks for a short time, is often regarded as a forerunner to modern France. To begin with, in 1066, William the Conqueror linked England and France, leading to centuries of hostility between them. In turn, Joan of

---

Arc (1412-1431) led France in expelling British soldiers before establishing today's France.

France Dominates (1500–1799)

France became one of Europe's major powers under Renaissance rulers François I and Henry IV, while Louis XIV elevated it to superpower status. During this period, French became the language spoken among well-educated people throughout Europe, and at the same time, their way of life was copied by Europeans, who pioneered aristocratic French customs everywhere.

Revolution (1789-1800)

On July 14th, 1789, revolutionaries stormed Bastille, resulting in the eventual execution of both the king and queen. Many were guillotined on suspicion as to whether or not they opposed democracy. From that maelstrom came Napoleon Bonaparte, a magnetic plebeian.

Elected Emperors and Constitutional Kings (1800s)

Napoleon would conquer much of Europe, including crowning himself emperor, before his disastrous invasion of Russia ended at Waterloo. Although monarchies had been reinstated, rulers had to take heed of democratic values. Later referred to as the belle époque or "beautiful age," this period saw grand monuments rise under Napoleon's nephew, Napoleon III, amongst other happenings such as the impressionist art explosion.

War and Depression (1900–1951)

Germany devastated France through two world wars. In the First World War, millions of Frenchmen were killed, while in the Second World War, Hitl*r quickly overwhelmed France. This period saw French writers like Hemingway and artists like Picasso flock to Paris due to its cheapness.

Postwar France (1950–Present)

After a wartime hero named Charles de Gaulle, France slowly rose again. Thus, as it lost its colonial heritage through wars such as those fought in Algeria and Vietnam, Paris found itself receiving immigrants. Turbulence characterized the 1960s, progress was made during the 1970s, socialism gave way to conservatism in the 1980s, and consensus reigned supreme in the 1990s, ushering in the 21st century. At present, Paris has become one of the world's leading cities once again.

Giverny

The garden of Claude Monet is still as beautiful as it was when he painted it. Go through the flowers, rose trellis, Japanese Bridge, and a pond filled with lily pads.

To get to Giverny, it is easiest to take a minivan or a bigger bus tour (€80–120). Another possibility is driving or taking a train from Gare St. Lazare to Vernon (about hourly, around €30 round-trip, 1 hour). From Vernon, you can either use a public bus that runs approximately every 2 hours (€10 round-trip), call a taxi (€20 one-way), or rent a bike at the café opposite the train station (closed Mondays).

Monet's Garden and House is open daily from 9:30–18:00, closed from November through late March (€11, not covered by the Museum Pass); ask about combo tickets with Paris' Orangerie or Marmottan Museums.

ACTIVITIES

To remain entertained, Paris provides numerous activities. Tours, shopping, and entertainment are the highlights of this chapter. The Seine River cruise is a great way to experience culture in a relaxed manner, or you can choose a leisurely bus tour. Bike and walking tours cover everything from classic art and architecture to unique topics like the history of the baguette.

Paris' market streets and village-like atmosphere are often overlooked by tourists rushing from museum to monument. Take some time off sightseeing to discover Parisian neighborhoods while living as locals do. Make sure you have enough energy left for exploring the City of Light after dark. This includes watching a concert at Sainte-Chapelle, taking a boat ride on the Seine, strolling through Montmartre, climbing the Arc de Triomphe, or visiting one of those cafés that never sleep to see how Paris does it.

Hop-On, Hop-Off Bus Tours: Paris' principal spots can be connected by double-decker buses, which offer an easy-to-follow city overview with basic recorded commentary. Just after alighting at any stop, enjoy exploring what is there, then hop onto another bus later. It's worth trying, as it may be quite picturesque if you get lucky with the weather when you're sitting on one of these seats on the top deck on the upper level, especially right now! However, due to heavy traffic conditions and frequent stops, they may run rather slowly sometimes. Busy tourists would prefer Métro lines instead (driver/ticket online/€36-39). The Toot Bus is central Paris's 10-stop route.

Seine Cruises: On the Seine River, different companies operate sixty-minute cruises whose ticket prices range from about €15–17 each way. For something special, choose an evening or twilight sail aboard one of these ships, returning home at midnight too, amongst other things like going past your eyes through famous bridges such as Pont d'Austerlitz while on board their boat "Bateaux-Mouche," which leaves from Pont de l'Alma and offers open-top double-decker boats (not recommended for claustrophobics, Bateaux-Mouches.fr). Bateaux Parisiens as well as Vedettes de Paris dock at the Eiffel Tower. Vedettes du Pont Neuf is located near Pont Neuf.

Walking Tours: These are two-hour engaging walks led by British or American guides at €15–25 per person. 2 times per day at www.paris-walks.com, and Context Travel provides private and small group walking tours for those serious about learning that cost around €120 per person and last about 3 hours per person.

Just some of the casual, fun Fat Tire Tours include their two-hour Classic Paris Walking Tour (Mon, Wed, and Fri at 10:00 or 15:00), while others, such as the Versailles Walking Tour (Mon, Wed, and Fri at 10:00 am) or the Sainte Chapelle Walking Tour (Tue-Sat; Sun at 2:30 pm and Mon at 11:15 am), get you into major attractions like Versailles, the Eiffel Tower, or the Catacombs, respectively, giving you a chance to skip lines in case you don't feel like waiting. The latter is located at Rue Edgar Faure, where only one person will be allowed in through the exit door; hence, it's advisable to take time before buying tickets since there are restrictions on how many people can enter this place simultaneously, and they also have some special offers like a discount worth €2 off each ticket up to a maximum of two discounts.

Connecting with the Culture

Paris is a place to meet and live with real French people throughout your stay; this makes the visit more personal and unforgettable. By meeting the French, travelers can connect with Parisians who offer specialized tours and trip-planning assistance. Volunteers at Paris Greeter give you personalized tours of "their Paris." The American Church in Paris and the Franco-American Center in the Rue Cler area offer numerous services for those wanting a taste of Parisian lifestyles. Lost in Frenchlation screens French films weekly with English subtitles. With local foodie experts leading small-group food tours, visitors will savor their way through Paris on various gourmet adventures offered by Paris by Mouth and learn how to cook traditional dishes during La Cuisine Paris' cooking classes, which are conducted mostly in English. Ô Château, wine-tasting sessions held at Madame de Pompadour's 18th-century residence.

Guides around

Some visitors find it worth paying for guided tours just to provide them with someone who knows their city (€240–300 per half day). www.french-guide.com.

Cycling Tours

Bike About Tours has easy rides lasting 3 hours and 30 minutes. While the Marais, Latin Quarter, and Ile St Louis are covered in Hidden Paris Tour Monuments, the Louvre, Eiffel Tower, and other similar attractions (€45 RS%—10 percent discount shop/café near Hôtel de Ville at 17 Rue du Pont Louis Philippe Mo: St-Paul Mobile +33 6 18 80 84 92 www.bikeabouttours.com).

Fat Tire provides three-hour bike trips around the streets of the French capital (€39–44; RS%—€4 discount per person, max save €8; at 10:30 April–October, also at 15:00). Their animated night rides take you past illuminated landmarks and include a boat cruise costing €44 May-August daily at 18:30. Office start locations: Fat Tire's office is located near the Eiffel Tower on Rue Edgar Faure (Mo: Dupleix or La Motte-Picquet-Grenelle, +33 1 82 88 80 96).

Shopping

Resisting temptation can be difficult when it comes to shopping in fashionable Paris. By checking out some chic boutiques, you can have a kind of interlude between visiting one museum and another. The French call it faire du lèche-vitrines, which means "window licking," but you may know it as window shopping.

Buying Tips and Manners

Whenever entering a little shop, say "Bonjour, Madame/Monsieur" to the shopkeeper and "Au revoir" when leaving. Watch the locals to see if self-service is allowed before purchasing anything. Always ask for permission before touching an item: "Je peux?" (zhuh puh), which means, "Can I?" There is no pressure to buy. If offered assistance, decline by saying, 'Je regarde, merci.' If you know what you want, point and say, 'S'il vous plaît' (please; see voo play). Note that smaller stores typically close on Sundays.

Shops with Souvenirs

Near Notre Dame, there are green riverfront stalls where second-hand books, vintage posters and postcards, magazines, and other souvenirs are sold in a romantic setting for tourists. Souvenir shops can also be found on Rue d'Arcole between Notre-Dame and Hôtel de Ville; across from the Louvre on Rue de Rivoli; around Pompidou Center; in Montmartre; and inside several department stores too.

Large Stores

Paris was not only cafés but also department stores first founded in France. Usually, information desks with floor plans in English are available near the main entrances next to the perfume section. These stores usually come with affordable restaurants, including some with terraces that are scenic, and a wide range of souvenirs at reasonable prices. The Galeries Lafayette flagship store at 40 Boulevard Haussmann is famed for its stunning Belle époque stained-glass dome and open-air rooftop view (https://haussmann.galerieslafayette.com). Nearby, Printemps offers more budget-friendly options and an equally impressive view.

Boutique Strolls

Place de la Madeleine Neighborhood: The luxurious mile of gourmet food shops, glittering jewelers, exclusive boutiques, and high-end hotels is located in an upscale street linking several posh squares: Place de la Madeleine, Place de la Concorde, Place Vendôme, and Place de l'Opéra. Start at Eglise de la Madeleine and go around the square in a counterclockwise direction. On the western side of the church, check out La Maison de la Truffe (#19) for a fragrant truffle experience; Mariage Frères (#17) sells premium teas; and Caviar Kaspia (#17) offers caviar, eel, and vodka. Where Fauchon's was once found on the north-east corner, there are other high-end shops to explore now. It is offered at Le Grand Café Fauchon's, which has a pink-and-black design with meals as well as pastries and a wine selection consisting of chocolates and gourmet groceries.

Extend your walk down Rue Royale; turn left on Rue St. Honoré (Ladurée at #16 is known for its macarons), then take another left onto Rue de Castiglione and finish up at the elegant Place Vendôme.

Sèvres-Babylone to St. Sulpice: To begin indulging in Left Bank sophistication, beginning with the historic Bon Marché department store. Pass La Maison du Chocolat at #19 on your way down Rue de Sèvres, and Hermès is on your right just before reaching it at #17 across from them. At 10 Rue de Sèvres, you'll be able to find Au Sauvignon Café, where fashion shoppers are noticed best by traditionists who cherish this café most of all. When going off-course via Rue du Cherche-Midi, you will realize that Paris' most famous bakery, Poilâne (8), is on the opposite side of the street. At Place St. Sulpice, one sees a twin-tower church and also Café de la Mairie, which is perfect for café crème with plans.

Flea Markets

Puces St. Ouen: Over 2,000 vendors here sell antiques, vintage items, and much more at Porte de Clignancourt; this is the ultimate flea market. This market represents the city's diverse culture. For some, it might be too crowded, while others love this fact about it (Sat 9:00–18:00, Sun 10:00–10:00, Mon 11:00–17:00, closed Tue-Fri.

From there, go straight in the direction of the elevated freeway towards Sortie Marché aux Puces, or just take Rue des Rosiers to the left.

Puces de Vanves: The latter offers a compact version of traditional markets (Sat-Sun 7:00–14:00, closed Mon–Fri; Mo: Porte de Vanves).

Traffic-Free Shopping

Rue Cler: A fancy market street (Mo: Ecole Militaire).

Rue Montorgueil: It is next to the Pompidou Center. These are the only remaining pieces of evidence of the historic Les Halles market (Mo: Etienne Marcel).

Rue Mouffetard: It starts at Place Contrescarpe, which is just behind Panthéon, and moving downhill, it becomes more Parisian. (Mo: Censier Daubenton).

Rue de Seine and Rue de Buci: Are central Left Bank market streets.

There is a marché volant ("flying market") in every district where producers sell their foodstuffs on certain boulevards or squares over one to three mornings a week, with cheeses, farm produce, wine, and trinkets.

VAT and Customs

Getting a VAT Refund: You can qualify for a 21% Value-Added Tax (VAT) refund if you spend more than €175 at one store. Find out from the trader.

Customs for American Shoppers: Americans are allowed to bring back $800 worth of merchandise per person every month duty-free and one liter of alcohol without paying duties. To get a clue on the goods, customs regulations, and rates, go to www.help.cbp.gov.

Nightlife

Paris comes alive after dusk. One of the best experiences during the nighttime is having a slow dinner followed by a walk through old streets in admiration of lit-up squares and fountains.

Jazz and Blues Clubs

Paris, which is famous for jazz music across the globe, has an amazing blend of American, French, and other international musicians performing locally. Jazz Club covers stand between €12 and €25. For timetables, go to the Paris Voice website, while Caveau de la Huchette (5 Rue de la Huchette, Mo: St-Michel, +33 1 43 26 65 05) provides night-time live jazz and dancing in an ancient Latin Quarter cellar. Au Duc des Lombards (42 Rue des Lombards, +33 1 42 33 22 88), which is among the city's most popular jazz clubs, holds nightly concerts in a plush theater setting, whereas Le Sunside (+33 1 40 26 46), located just meters away, features two small stages.

Classical Concerts

Churches like St. Sulpice, St. Germain-des-Prés, La Madeleine, St. Eustache, St. Julien-le-Pauvre, and Sainte-Chapelle host regular concerts mainly with Baroque chamber music throughout the spring until the autumn season. The latter's eight-century-old stained-glass backdrop magnificently illustrates some works by Vivaldi Bach or Mozart (it's unheated; bring a sweater; 8 Boulevard du Palais, Mo: Cité, +33 1 42 77 65 65).

Opera

The Opéra Bastille is known for its contemporary productions and state-of-the-art special effects. The historic Opéra Garnier, the original opera house in Paris, still stages opera as well as ballet amid great Belle époque surroundings. Therefore, one can get tickets via the Internet for both places.

Evening Sightseeing

Some museums, such as Pompidou, Orsay, and Marmottan, and sometimes the Louvre, remain open late on certain nights called visites nocturnes when you can have a more relaxed and less crowded experience. At Versailles, there is an elaborate sound-and-light show in the gardens on some Saturday evenings during the summer (Les Grandes Eaux Nocturnes).

Tours by Night

In this case, consider a Seine River cruise in the evening or take it to another level with a bus tour. Two companies operate informal tours on old Deux Chevaux cars that carry up to three people each: Paris

Authentic and 4 Roues Sous 1 Parapluie. Otherwise, hop into a taxi or Uber for your scenic tour from Notre Dame to the Eiffel Tower along the Left Bank and back along the Right Bank at around €50 for a one-hour taxi loop or €40 by Uber.

Night Scenes

Place du Trocadéro, from where hawkers, sightseers, and performers abound at night, gives you a picturesque view of the Eiffel Tower, which is also breathtaking from the Champs-Elysées towards the Arc de Triomphe after dark, while Ile St. Louis (Mo: Pont Marie) offers peaceful romantic dining spots with ice creams available before taking a casual walk to Notre Dame Cathedral.

The Left Bank can be experienced by visiting the areas around Saint-Germain-des-Prés and Odéon, both filled with famous bistros, movie theaters, and bohemians along Rue des Canettes, Rue Guisarde, or Rue de Buci. Although touristy, Montmartre does not lose its life, even if it is a bit dangerous at night. To have a taste of an old-style afternoon music hall, think about going to Au Lapin Agile (€35, French only shows), located at 22 rue des Saules (tel. 01 46 06 85 87), and end up in front of the Sacré-Cœur Basilica.

SLEEPING

The proper choice of district is as essential as picking the right hotel in Paris. My recommendation would be to focus on three lively and safe areas: the lovely Rue Cler (near the Eiffel Tower), the trendy and creative Marais (close to Place de la Bastille), and the lively, elegant Luxembourg (in Left Bank). Moreover, I mention a few alternatives on Ile St. Louis, Rue Mouffetard, and Montmartre. I prefer clean accommodations that are centrally located, relatively quiet at night, reasonably priced, welcoming, small enough for a hands-on owner or manager, and run with French customs in mind.

Double rooms in this guide average around €130–200 (with private bathrooms). These prices can vary from about €70 (basic; shared toilet and shower) to €400 (luxury options with extensive amenities).

Paris Hotels

Book your lodgings well in advance, especially during peak travel periods or major holidays. For hotels, prices differ based on room size, whether a bathroom has a bathtub or only a shower and bed configuration (rooms with tubs and twin beds usually cost more than those with showers and double beds). If you do not mind, what sort of room do you get asked for? Standard "Chambre pour deux" (room for two?)

Elevators are frequent fixtures in Parisian hotels, but they could be tiny, while some older ones lack elevators altogether. Most rooms have television sets and free Wi-Fi, but signal strength may differ.

Hotels typically offer breakfast; however, it is rarely included in the price of the room (usually between €10 and €20). In general, there is cereal, fruit, yogurt, cheese, ham, croissants, juice, boiled eggs, coffee, and a self-service buffet.

Instead of being based on overall quality rather than anything else such as better lobbies or designs of rooms, the French hotel rating system spans from zero stars up to five stars depending on how many extra features are present.

Making Reservations

Once you have confirmed the dates of your journey, make sure to book where you will be staying ahead of time. Talk to them through their email address or phone number. You may also visit their official website to do so. Be sure to give the hotelier your contact details:

Type of room(s) needed and the number of guests.

Duration of stay.

Check-in and check-out dates in the European format (day/month/year, e.g., 18/06/25 or 18 June 2025).

Special requests (e.g., en suite bathroom, budget room, twin vs. double bed, quiet location).

Any applicable discounts (like promotional offers or special rates).

Most hotels will ask for a credit card number to secure your booking. If the hotel's website doesn't have a secure form, provide your details over the phone.

If you need to cancel, it's polite and wise to do so with ample notice. Cancellation policies can be strict, so read the terms carefully. Always reconfirm your reservation a few days before arrival. Select chambres d'hôtes or choose small hotels, I call it, again on the day of arrival to inform the host of my expected time (especially if arriving after 17:00).

Sleep Code

Dollar signs represent the average price for a standard double room without breakfast during high season.

Price Range	Description	Cost
$$$$	Splurge: Most rooms over	€300
$$$	Pricier:	€200-300
$$	Moderate:	€130-200
$	Budget:	€70-130
¢	Backpacker: Under	€70

French hotel rating system (0-5 stars)

If nothing is said, credit cards are accepted, and some members of staff can speak English while free Wi-Fi access is provided.

Budget Tips

Check Prices: Visit their websites, and use booking platforms or email services to compare charges of several hotels. To get the best deals, go to the hotel itself and ask if they offer cash discounts.

Consider Location: Opting for accommodations further from the river can yield lower rates and more options but expect to spend extra time traveling to major attractions.

Look Into Apartments: If you're staying for several nights, especially with a group or family, an apartment might be more economical. For instance in Europe, apartments are quite small as compared to those in the US however; most of them have laundry facilities as well as fully equipped kitchens. Airbnb, FlipKey, Booking.com, and VRBO are some of the websites where one can find listings and communicate directly with property owners.

Rue Cler area Accommodations

A chic yet safe district that is well-maintained near the Eiffel Tower. They include Ecole Militaire, La Tour Maubourg, and Invalides.

$$$$ Splurge: Most rooms over €300

Hôtel du Cadran****

Modern slick close Rue Cler, with a wine bar in the lobby. Designer rooms." 10 Rue du Champ de Mars +33 1 40 62 67 00.

Hôtel de Latour-Maubourg***

A tranquil manor setting with plush, spacious rooms (17), a small patio, and free spa access for guests. 150 Rue de Grenelle +33 1 47 05 16 16.

$$$ Pricy: €200-300

Hôtel de Londres Eiffel****

Closest to the Eiffel Tower and Champ de Mars Park, immaculate, warmly decorated rooms welcome public spaces and family rooms. The address is 1 Rue Augereau +33 1 45 51 63 02.

Cler Hotel***

Small outdoor patio, charming decor, superb location on Rue Cler, well-designed rooms. They are located at 24 bis Rue Cler +33 1 45 00 18 06.

Hôtel Relais Bosquet***

Prime location, comfortable public areas, spacious by Paris standards. The address is 19 Rue du Champ de Mars +33 1 47 05 25 45.

Hôtel de la Motte Picquet***

Cozy hotel on the corner of Rue Cler and Avenue de la Motte-Picquet. The staff is nice, the breakfast is okay, the bike rental is easy, and the family room exists. The exact address is 30 Avenue de la Motte-Picquet, +33 1 47 05 09 57.

Hôtel de l'Empereur***

Luxurious with stunning Invalides views from many rooms, all equipped with queen or king beds. Some have views; family rooms are available. 2 Rue Chevert +33 (0)145558802.

Hôtel Eiffel Turenne***

Well-maintained, sharp rooms, friendly lounge, service-oriented staff. 20 Avenue de Tourville, +33 (0)147059992.

Hôtel Muguet***

Quiet, good value for money, located near main sights, tastefully furnished rooms, helpful staff, and some offer views. 11 rue Chevert +33 (0)147050593

Hôtel les Jardins d'Eiffel***

This is a large hotel situated on a quiet street; there is no personalized service here since it has a serene patio and consists of eighty-one well-configured rooms with partial views of the Eiffel Tower and balconies. 8 Rue Amélie +33 (0)147054621.

Hôtel de la Paix***

Quiet Lane intimately and tastefully designed six true singles. Address is 19 Rue du Gros Caillou +33 (0)145518617.

$$ Moderate: €130-200

Hôtel du Champ de Mars***

Exceptionally located just off Rue Cler, snug yet charming rooms are maintained by hands-on owner Céline. Some well-priced singles. Continental breakfast only. 7 rue du champ de mars +33 (0)145515230.

Hôtel Duquesne Eiffel***

It is a beautiful and hospitable place with pleasant rooms (some with breathtaking views of the Eiffel Tower), a cozy lobby for receiving guests, a facade terrace street, and family accommodations. 23 Avenue Duquesne, +33 1 44 42 09.

Hôtel Beaugency*

There are thirty small rooms, many of which have double beds. The hotel has a spacious lobby and street that offer good value. 21 Rue Duvivier, +33 1 47 05 01 63.

$ Budget: €70-130

Hôtel de la Tour Eiffel**

This place provides good value for money on a quiet road with plain but well-laid-out and air-conditioned spaces. Their connecting rooms are suitable for those who come as families. It is located at No. 17 Rue de l'Exposition, +33 1 47 O5 I4 75.

Hôtel Kensington**

A moderately pocket-friendly choice near the Eiffel Tower with few luxuries; others have partial views of the tower. There's no AC or heat, but there are fans in the ceilings. 79 Avenue de la Bourdonnais, +33.1.47.05.74.00.

Marais area Accommodations

Greenwich Village-like is what the elegant mansions and chic boutiques are all about. Metro stations nearby include St-Paul, Bastille, and Hôtel de Ville.

$$$ Expensive: €200-300

Hôtel Bastille Spéria****

Which is only a block away from Place de la Bastille and provides professional services and comfort. Its location is busy, and the 42 rooms have modern furnishings. Find it at 1 Rue de la Bastille, +33 1 42 72 04 01.

Hotel Castex***

On a peaceful street close to Place de la Bastille, there are linked family rooms consisting of tiny tiled spaces for families. It lies just off Place de la Bastille and Rue St. Antoine at number five, Rue Castex, +33 1 42-72-31 -52.

The Hôtel St. Louis Marais***

Is a small, refined hotel on a quiet street near the river. The rooms are stylish, with large bathrooms. Visit it at 1 Rue Charles V, Mo.: Sully-Morland, +33 1 48 87 87 04.

Hôtel Saint-Louis***

Has shabby-chic rooms with stone floors and exposed beams. The rates are quite reasonable for the location. Located at 75 Rue St. Louis-en-l'Ile, +33 1 46 34 04 80.

Hotel de Lutèce***

Is inviting with its paneled wood walls and traditional rooms having wood beam ceilings. There are high ceilings in the lower-floor rooms; bathtubs in the streetside ones; and showers in the courtyard ones. Located at number sixty-five Rue St. Louis-en-l'Ile, +33 (0)143262352.

$$ Moderate: €130-200

Hôtel Jeanne d'Arc***

With its interior of stone walls and oak floors, it has an amazing position in town. The corner rooms are bright while street-facing ones can be noisier. Family rooms are available; there is no air conditioning. It is located at number three, Rue de Jarente, +33 (0)148876211.

Hôtel Beaubourg ***

offers great deals on a tiny street close to Centre Pompidou. It is tranquility itself, with plush traditional rooms numbering twenty-eight. The best deal is for larger doubles. Find it at number eleven, Rues Simon Le Franc, Mo.: Rambuteau, +33 (0)142743424.

Hôtel de la Bretonnerie***

Has a cozy reception area with friendly staff. The larger side has thirty good-value rooms, including family ones. No air-conditioning. Located at twenty-two Rue St. Croix de la Bretonnerie, +33 (0)148877763.

The Hôtel de Neuve**

Is a small, nice place that is central but unpretentious, with quiet, pleasant rooms that represent good value for money in a pricey area. Twin rooms have tub showers and are slightly bigger. It's situated on fourteen Rue de Neuve, +33 (0)144592850.

$ Budget: €70-130

Sully Hotel*

Provides basic accommodation in Paris with simple, modernized interiors. Good value for budget travelers. Family rooms are available. There is no elevator, no air conditioning, and no breakfast. It can be found on forty-eight Rue St. Antoine; phone +(331) 42784932.

¢ Backpacker: Under €70

MIJE Fourcy ¢

Is a former historical house that now serves as a budget hotel. Cheap dinners are available with a membership card. No air-conditioning. It is located at 6 Rue de Fourcy, south of Rue de Rivoli, +33 1 42 74 23 45.

MIJE Fauconnier ¢

Is there a sister hostel to MIJE Fourcy that offers similar services without an elevator? Located at 11 Rue du Fauconnier, +33 1 42 74 23 45.

Luxembourg Garden area Accommodations

The area has a Left Bank feel with lively shops, cafes, and a famous park close by. Metro stations in the vicinity include Cluny-La Sorbonne, St. Sulpice, Mabillon, and Odéon.

$$$$ Spend: Over €300

Hôtel de l'Abbaye****

Is a charming retreat just west of Luxembourg Garden. It has four stars and an intimate sitting area outside and inside, with 44 well-furnished rooms that offer all the amenities required for a luxurious stay. You will find it at 10 Rue Cassette, +33 1 45 44 38 11.

Hôtel le Récamier****

Is positioned romantically on the corner of Place St. Sulpice. It also boasts designer common places, opulently decorated bedrooms, a courtyard tea salon, and free tea and bites in the afternoons. The place offers top-notch customer service as well as some family rooms that have connecting doors. Go to www.hotelrecamier.com or call +33 1 43 26 04 89 for more information.

$$$ Expensive: €200-300

Hôtel Signature St. Germain-des-Prés****

On a quiet road near the fashionable Sèvres-Babylone shopping area is St. Germain-des-Prés, which creates a cool atmosphere similar to its neighboring boutiques. The hotel includes some staff who are very nice people, along with about twenty-six other rooms that come in different color designs, including some balconies, making them suitable for families too. Mo: Sèvres-Babylone, where this hotel is located, is found at address number five, Rue Chomel; +33 1 45 48 35 53.

Hôtel Victoire et Germain****

It is one of our favorite hotels, located just steps from Boulevard St. Germain and Rue de Buci because it offers Scandinavian comfort mixed with a touch of modernism under white beams. It is located at 9 Rue Grégoire de Tours, +33 1 45 49 03 26.

Hôtel Relais Médicis****

Is just what you need for those who want to experience Monet's picture in reality. It has a glass-covered entrance that leads to its seventeen rooms that surround the courtyard garden and fountain, which fills the air with a sweet fragrance. The rooms are tasteful yet practical, complete with family room options. Located at 5 Place de l'Odéon, +33 1 43 26 00 60.

Odéon Hôtel***

It has a large lobby lounge, dim hallways, and old-world-styled rooms that have all the luxury required for your stay. It is located at number three, rue de l'Odéon; +33 1-43-25-90-76.

Hôtel des Marronniers***

Situated on a quiet street, it combines Old World charm with modern comfort. The atrium breakfast room, lovely garden courtyard, cozy lounges, and plush rooms are among its features. You'll find it at this address: 21 Rue Jacob; +33 1 43 25 30.

Hôtel Relais St. Sulpice***

It is situated on a small street behind St. Sulpice Church. This hotel provides an intimate lounge and twenty-six artsy bedrooms, most of which are glass-roofed leafy courtyards. The ones facing the streets receive more light, while those looking inside are quieter as they face into the courtyard itself, along with a free sauna for guests' use. Located at Rue Garancière.

$$ Affordable: €130-200

Hôtel Bonaparte***

Is a modest hotel that offers warm hospitality. The decor is plain, the rooms are big, and the staff is very friendly. 61 Rue Bonaparte, +33 1 43 26 97 37, www.hotelbonaparte.fr.

Hôtel Michelet Odéon**

Occupies a corner of Place de l'Odéon with expansive windows overlooking the place. These rooms have trendy hues but no fancy frills. The service here is non-interacting, but there are family quarters on offer. No air conditioning. 6 Place de l'Odéon, +33 1 53 10 05 60.

$ Cheap: €70-130

Hôtel Jean Bart**

Is truly an economic discovery in this neighborhood, as it is situated just one block away from Luxembourg Garden. With poor lighting in the lobby, all of the thirty-three rooms are more or less comfortable, and some have small bathrooms where floors creak a lot. They also provide breakfast without air conditioning. 9 Rue Jean-Bart, +33 1 45 48 29 13.

EATING

The Parisian dining scene is perpetually alive with buzz. It has had countless tomes (and even entire lives) penned about it, and trendy chefs are often pursued by journalists. City dwellers are known for their long, leisurely meals. Long lunches, three-hour dinners, and endless hours spent at outdoor cafés are typical. Save some cash—and time—to taste the flavors of Paris. If you're in a budget hotel, don't deprive yourself of a first-class experience.

I have various restaurants that are all diverse in style, from quick bites that cater to people on tight budgets to those offering multicourse meals in elegant environments. My recommendations can be found in the lovely neighborhoods of Paris, which conveniently sit next to highly recommended hotels and attractions.

While in France...

I follow the local eating schedule. I either eat at the hotel or get a café au lait and croissant at a café counter for breakfast. Lunch (12:00–14:30) could be any one of a hearty salad, a plat du jour, or an idyllic picnic. In the late afternoon, Parisians enjoy a drink at a sidewalk café. Dinner is one point where I slow down and enjoy my multi-course meal.

Restaurants

Many open around 19:00 (as early as 18:30), and some may be very busy by 21:00. French cafes and restaurants usually close on Sundays and/or Mondays. Outdoor tables can have smokers, while the interiors of cafés and restaurants do not permit smoking.

A full French dinner consists of many different courses. Aperitif (drink before dinner), entrée (appetizer), plat principal (main course), cheese plate, dessert, coffee, liqueurs/hard drinks/cocktails, and several wines. This can be done à la carte (ordering individual dishes) or by choosing a fixed-priced multicourse menu, which is confusingly called a "menu." Alternatively, there is always a menu instead of a la carte, which is a fixed-price meal.

It is not necessary to order every course; some Parisians consider a full meal to be two courses (for example, main and dessert). One can just order a main course. Two people may have an appetizer or a big salad (small dinner salads are rarely available à la carte), and each then chooses a main course. A café or brasserie will do for only soup or salad.

Most restaurants offer menus with two dishes, often called formulas that include starter-main or main-dessert. Drinks and certain premium items cost extra, as indicated on the menu (supplément or sup.). Bottled water (eau minérale) is usually charged at Parisian restaurants, although you can always ask for tap water in a carafe for free (une carafe d'eau). Bread is complimentary.

Cafés and restaurants typically include service charges in the bill, so additional tipping is not expected, but of course, you can tip if you wish to reward very good service. You see that French waiters don't strive to be too friendly.

To get your waiter's attention, look them in the eye and raise your hand, saying, "S'il vous plaît." This same phrase applies when calling for the bill: "L'addition, s'il vous plaît." In France, servers generally do not bring the check until asked; it would be considered rude had they brought it unsolicited because it shows forwardness in their culture.

Restaurant Code

Dollar symbols represent the price of a typical main course.

Symbol	Description	Price Range
$$$$	Splurge	Most main courses over €40
$$$	Pricier	€30-40
$$	Moderate	€20-30
$	Budget	Under €20

The ratings of dining establishments in France fall into the following categories: $ for a crêpe stand or other takeout option; $$ to $$$ for sit-down brasseries, cafés, and bistros with reasonably priced plats du jour; and $$$$ for high-end dining experiences.

To fully enjoy dining in France, take your time. Embrace the leisurely French dining pace, interact with the waitstaff, show your appreciation for good food, and then savor the experience as much as you savor the cuisine itself. Bon appétit.

Cafés and Brasseries

Less formal than traditional restaurants, these places offer relaxed meals along with coffee and drinks. They serve food throughout the day so that you can order just a salad, sandwich, or bowl of soup even in the evening. While main dishes are rarely shared, one may share starters and desserts.

Feel free to choose a plat (main course), plat du jour (daily special), salad (usually generous in size), sandwich (like a croque monsieur or grilled ham sandwich), omelet fish fry (appetizer), or soup bowl. Most have outdoor seating areas suitable even when fitted with heaters during winter when one can sip wine or café au lait while observing others go by. Another informal, budget-friendly option is a crêperie where sweet dessert crêpes and savory meal-style ones are available too.

Prices vary depending on your seating choice; you will pay more for the same drink if you are at a table (salle) than at the bar or counter (Comptoir).

Picnicking

Picnicking in Paris might easily turn into a gourmet experience. Takeout delis (charcuteries or traiteurs plus some bakeries) give cooked dishes such as quiches, pâtés, small pizzas, salads, etc. to make up lunch around them; they reheat it all (chauffé) and pack it in a takeout box (une barquette) with a plastic fork (fourchette).

For sides, a generic supermarché is convenient for one-stop shopping, but you'll find better quality at a boulangerie for your baguette, a fromagerie for cheese, and an open-air market for the freshest produce.

Have no fear. Sample some pungent cheeses, unusual pâtés, as well as minuscule little yogurts. The best places to picnic in central Paris are the Palais Royal courtyard, Place des Vosges, the western tip of the île de la cité, and the Tuileries Garden.

French Cuisine

You can embark on a culinary journey across France without leaving Paris because the city's restaurants offer diverse regional specialties.

Though many serve French food in general, some are more committed to dishes from particular regions of France.

From Burgundy, known for some of France's finest cuisine, comes coq au vin, or chicken cooked in red wine sauce, bœuf bourguignon, or beef stew, and escargot snails. Normandy and Brittany bring you mussels, oysters, crepes, cider, and others, while dishes labeled à la provençale savor garlic, olive oil, herbs, and tomatoes from Provence. From Côte d'Azur, we have bouillabaisse; foie gras from the southwest; Alsatian choucroute—sauerkraut.

Parisians are very fond of steak, including raw delicacies like steak tartare. Other popular choices include confit de canard (duck from Dordogne), gigot d'agneau (leg of lamb), poulet rôti (roasted chicken), and saumon (salmon). At Christmas, raw oysters from Brittany (huîtres) form part of their diet. Five classic French sauces include béchamel made with milk espagnole based on veal, velouté made from stock, tomato, which is based on tomatoes, and hollandaise made with egg yolk.

Cheese, another head-turner, has a menu that includes Brie de Meaux (soft and creamy from close to Paris), Camembert (semi-creamy and pungent from Normandy), chèvre, and Roquefort In many restaurants, you can get a plate of cheese.

For dessert, go for Café Gourmand, which is an assortment of small recommendations by the restaurant. Other common ones include crème brûlée, tarte tatin, and mousse au chocolat.

No French meal would be complete without wine. Even simple table wines or vin du pays to pair well with food—ask for it by the 'picket' or pitcher. For good, inexpensive bottles, try reds from Côtes du Rhône or Languedoc and whites from Burgundy or Alsace; in summer, a refreshing rosé is just right; if you want to splurge, try a pinot noir from Burgundy or any strong red wine from Bordeaux.

The French generally do not imbibe wine as an apéritif drink. Instead, they prefer champagne, beer, Kir (white wine mixed with crème de cassis), or Pastis (aniseed-flavored liquor originating in Provence). The best French beers, such as Kronenbourg 1664 and the stronger Pelfort, are produced in Alsace. A panaché of lemon soda mixed with beer is a perfect choice on a hot day.

Parisians usually order (un café espresso macchiato), une noisette (espresso with just a splash of milk), and café au lait/café crème (espresso with steamed milk). An interesting non-alcoholic beverage is un diabolo menthe, which is 7-up mixed with mint syrup. If ordering Coke, though, remember that ice cubes are seldom used in Paris.

Rue Cler area

Where to Eat Near the Eiffel Tower (for Locals and Tourists alike) with Metro Stop: Ecole Militaire, La Tour-Maubourg.

$$$$ Le Violon d'Ingres: This is a Michelin-starred restaurant offering fine dining with a seven-course tasting menu (€150) or à la carte options. Lunch is cheaper, and reservations are necessary. 135 Rue St. Dominique, +33 1 45 55 15 05.

$$$ La Fontaine de Mars: A favorite neighborhood place on a charming square that is good for superb foie gras and desserts (daily; reserve ahead for ground floor or patio tables). 129 Rue St. Dominique, +33 1 47 05 46 44.

$$$ Au Petit Tonneau Quaint: This is a French bistro with an old-world feel that has seasonal menus and reasonably priced wines. This is away from the tourist rush of Rue Cler, which closes except Mondays off-season. 20 Rue Surcouf, +33 1 47 05 09 01.

$$$ Bistrot Belhara: It's not just about the food itself but also about the intimate setting in vintage French style where you can get traditional dishes at affordable prices (closed Sun-Mon. reservations recommended). 23 Rue Duvivier, +33 1 45 51 41.

$$ Le Septième Vin: This is an intimate spot with great traditional food and a romantic Paris atmosphere (closed on Sundays). 68 Avenue Bosquet, +33-145511597.

$$ La Terrasse du Septieme: Is a vibrant café with an extensive outdoor seating area as well as comfortable inside seating that does not fail to offer good salads, French onion soup, and liver pate (daily until midnight). 2 Place de L'Ecole Militaire, +33-145550002.

$$ Café le Bosquet: modern brasserie with fair pricing and standard café dishes like salads, French onion soup, and steak-frites (closed Sundays). 46 Avenue Bosquet, +33-145513813.

$$ Le P'tit Troquet: This small place reminds us of Paris in the 1920s with traditional meals served in a cozy manner and dinner for €40 with three courses (closed Sun; reservations recommended). 28 Rue de l'Exposition, +33 1 47 05 80 39.

$$ Café de Mars: A calm spot where you can find globally inspired items with creative names that are vegetarian-friendly (closed Sunday-Mon). 11 Rue Augereau, +33-145501090.

$ Café du Marché: Just a few blocks down on the same street is Café du Marche, which offers affordable one-course meals, hearty salads, and daily specials. On most evenings after seven, it tends to get crowded, but the food remains good (daily). 38 Rue Cler, +33-147055127.

$ Le Petit Cler: Popular bistro with vintage decor, offering inexpensive plates in a cozy setting (daily). 29 Rue Cler.

$ Le Royal: A small place in the neighborhood where ordinary things are done at prices and décor that seem to belong to another time completely (closed Sundays). 212 Rue de Grenelle, +33-147539290.

$ Crep' and Tea: Creative menu featuring homemade crêpes in a tidy, shoebox-sized room with Tetris-like seating (open daily). 139 Rue St. Dominique, +33 1 45 51 70 78.

The hottest spots within the lively nightlife scene. Metro stations: Chemin Vert, St-Paul, Hôtel de Ville, or Bastille.

$$ La Place Royale: A traditional menu in a top location on Place des Vosges is perfect for an unhurried meal with generous food and a good choice of wine (daily, reserve for outdoor seating). 2 bis Place des Vosges, +33 1 42 78 58 16.

$$ Chez Janou: French Mediterranean dishes served in Provençal bistro style; famous for its animated café culture and friendliness towards guests (daily, book ahead or arrive early). 2 Rue Roger Verlomme, +33 1 42 72 28 41.

$$ Le Petit Marché: Friendly service and delicious cuisine in this warm bistro with some Asian flavors mixed with French classics (daily, book a day ahead). 9 Rue du Béarn, +33 1 42 72 06 67.

$$ Brasserie Bofinger: The grand interior décor reflects the Alsatian foods and seafood that it is known for but also has the Roaring Twenties feel (daily for lunch and dinner). 5 Rue de la Bastille, +33-142728782.

$ Café Hugo: simple café fare and salads amidst the vibrant Parisian ambiance located under the arches of Place des Vosges. The place is open daily. 22 Place des Vosgues +33 (0)1.42.72.64.04

An ideal place to pass an evening leisurely; romantically serene. Metro station: Pont Marie.

$$$ Chez Fernand: This cramped eatery serves robust classical bistro meals in the colorful ambiance of tightly packed tables covered by red checkered tablecloths (opens at 19:00, closed Mon.).13 Rue Guisarde, +33143546147.

$$$ Les Deux Magots and Café de Flore: The historical Parisian cafés have been frequented by known personalities. Les Deux Magots—6 Place St. Germain-des-Prés, +33 1 45 48 55 25. Café de Flore—172 Boulevard St. Germain-des-Prés, +33 1 45 48 55 26.

$$ Monte Verdi: Located in several rooms with live piano accompaniment for each room, this is an Italian restaurant (closed Sun).5 Rue Guisarde, +33142345590.

$$ Nos Ancêtres les Gaulois: A medieval cellar atmosphere marks this boisterous eatery with an all-you-can-eat menu at €40 per person (daily). 39 Rue St. Louis en l'Ile, +33146336607.

$$ Les Deux Palais: It has a bistro atmosphere and dates back to the year of France's defeat in the Franco-Prussian war; there are moderate charges and professional staff; it is ideal for lunch or a tea break while doing sightseeing as it faces Sainte-Chapelle (daily until 11:00). 3 Boulevard du Palais, +33134542086.

$$ Les Fous de l'Ile: This fun bistro offers gourmet food at reasonable prices, with two- or three-course menus or plat du jour (daily). 33 Rue des Deux Ponts, +33143257667.

$$ L'Orangerie: This inviting yet rustic place is elegantly designed to combine traditional and modern tastes in its dishes, served in quiet surroundings that make you feel comfortable (closed Mon.).28 Rue St. Louis en l'Ile, +33185152131.

$ Restaurant Polidor: Since 1845, this favorite Parisian café has maintained an old-time bustling allure with long shared tables and serves traditional dishes from all over France (daily reservations recommended). 41 Rue Monsieur le Prince, +33143269534.

$ Auberge de la Reine Blanche: A cozy eatery with a tiny dining space in the wood; that serves simple French food at reasonable charges; excellent dinner salads; and an attentive owner, Michel (opens 18:30 and closed Monday). 30 Rue St. Louis en l'Ile, +33185152130.

SAFETY AND EMERGENCIES

Emergency and Medical Help

In case of an emergency such as an ambulance, police, or fire, dial **112** on any telephone. In case you get sick, the French will often visit a chemist for advice or at their hotel to assist in finding the nearest medical help.

These are some places with staff that speak English:

American Hospital (63 Boulevard Victor Hugo, +33 1 46 41 25 25, www.american-hospital.org).

Pharmacie des Champs (84 Avenue des Champs-Elysées, Mo: George V, +33 1 45 62 02 41).

Pharmacie Anglaise (62 Avenue des Champs-Elysées, +33 1 43 59 82 30).

Theft or Loss

Though Paris is safe from violent crime to some extent, it is infested with pickpockets and con artists who prey on tourists. Beware of smartphone theft, particularly on the metro and during crowded events. Keep your phone out of sight, and think about using a money belt. Put your wallet in your front pocket instead of your back pocket; sling your bag crosswise over your shoulder with a firm grip on it. If you lose your passport, you should go to the American Embassy (+33-1-43-12-22-22) personally, with its address being near Hotel Crillon at

No. 2 Avenue Gabriel in Missouri. If your credit card or ATM card gets stolen, just close them down immediately.

Here are some US numbers open around the clock:

Visa: +1-303-967-1096

MasterCard: +1-636-722-7111

American Express: +1-3363931111

To recover lost items, one can reach the Bureau des Objets Trouvés on Mon-Fri from eight-thirty to five p.m. GMT, excluding weekends and holidays, located at the police station on 36 Rue des Morillons, Mo: Convention, +33 1 53 71 53 71.

Street Smarts

Cross streets with caution even though it appears there are no cars or other vehicles on the way, e.g., bicycles, buses, and taxis, among others. You cannot expect to be treated with regard by Parisian drivers since they usually disregard pedestrians, thinking that they already know everything, so do not cross a street assuming you have priority, even if it's a pedestrian walkway. It is important to be alert for cyclists who ride on sidewalks marked for bike lanes as well as regular traffic bus or taxi lanes. Check both sides of one-way streets because bicycles can go in the opposite direction.

CONCLUSION

I appreciate this walk-through of Paris. The Travel Guide to Paris is a work of passion that has been inspired by the city's enduring beauty, active lifestyle, and historical tradition. I trust you will find it useful in making your stay in Paris more fruitful.

Paris is a place that is always amazing, where there are landmarks known worldwide, secrets, and diverse neighborhoods. Be it inside Louvres, eating croissants at some café, or along the Seine River when dusk breaks, no other place can you get such an experience as Paris.

Allow yourself to feel the heartbeat of the city and not just run through its streets. One does not have strong memories about these places but for those extra moments spent between the main attractions, such as getting lost on the little streets of Le Marais, stumbling upon a nice café, or just sitting in a park and seeing people pass by,.

I hope this guide gives you the confidence to navigate and love Paris. Enjoy your time in the City of Lights, which will be filled with unforgettable experiences that will remain memorable.

Thank you so much for using my book during your journey through France! Have a great journey through beautiful Paris!

Best regards,

Etienne Cartier

Made in the USA
Las Vegas, NV
02 August 2024

93264157R00105